with the authors
on his seven[illegible]
birthday
Jan 4 · 1923 ·

EIGHT CHAPTERS
ON
ENGLISH MEDIEVAL ART

CAMBRIDGE UNIVERSITY PRESS
C. F. CLAY, Manager
LONDON : FETTER LANE, E.C. 4

NEW YORK : THE MACMILLAN CO.
BOMBAY, CALCUTTA, MADRAS : MACMILLAN AND CO., Ltd.
TORONTO : THE MACMILLAN CO. OF CANADA, Ltd.
TOKYO : MARUZEN-KABUSHIKI-KAISHA

Plate I

THIRTEENTH CENTURY PAINTING
(Bishop's Chapel, Chichester)

EIGHT CHAPTERS
ON
ENGLISH MEDIEVAL ART
A STUDY IN ENGLISH ECONOMICS

BY

E. S. PRIOR, A.R.A.

SLADE PROFESSOR OF FINE ART IN THE UNIVERSITY OF CAMBRIDGE

CAMBRIDGE
AT THE UNIVERSITY PRESS
1922

PRINTED IN GREAT BRITAIN

PREFACE

THESE chapters in their substance are the "Carpenter" Lectures as they were given to University College, London, in 1911. Recast for Cambridge students—specially for the English Tripos—they aim at being a general review of the Church-Building Arts of England. Art-craftsmanship, in its power of recording social and economic history, is unfamiliar to our practice of art which knows only its taste and design. This book ventures to stress the facts, which bear on the economy of architecture and are necessary for the understanding of the medieval records.

Since good photographic illustration of the English monuments is abundant it has not been thought necessary to repeat the well-known views. Mr S. Gardner has lately published his fine photographs of English churches, that he has allowed me to use for my lectures: they are referred to here under Roman numerals. Mr Arthur Gardner's plates of English Sculpture appear in our book published in 1912, and are also cited for reference. The student is referred to other illustrations in the works of Sir T. G. Jackson, Professor Baldwin Brown and the late Francis Bond. The author begs to acknowledge his indebtedness to their views and drawings, to Dr Cranage and Mr Cyril Fox for looking through his proofs, to Messrs G. Bell and Sons for the loan of blocks, and to the authorities of the National Museums for the use of their photographs.

The ancient building itself is the best study for the reader, but its art is cited here with the caution, that it is now overlaid with glosses and restorations, and that the new work must necessarily lack the craft competence which made the old the vehicle of medieval civilization.

E. S. P.

July 1922.

CONTENTS

CHAP. I. THE BEGINNINGS, TO 1080

LIST OF ILLUSTRATIONS

NOTE

The references for illustration are mainly to the following:

A Guide to English Gothic Architecture, S. Gardner. Camb. Univ. Press, 1922.

Medieval Figure-Sculpture in England, E. S. Prior and A. Gardner. Camb. Univ. Press, 1912.

History of Gothic Art in England, E. S. Prior and G. Horsley. G. Bell and Sons, 1900.

Cathedral Builders, E. S. Prior. Seeley and Co. 1905.

Byzantine and Romanesque Architecture, T. G. Jackson. Camb. Univ. Press, 1913.

Gothic Architecture, T. G. Jackson. Camb. Univ. Press, 1915.

Gothic Architecture in England, Francis Bond. Batsford, 1905.

English Church Architecture, Francis Bond. Milford, 1913.

Other authorities are cited on pages as under:

For Chapter I.

Baldwin Brown, *The Arts of Early England*, Vol. I. 3, 4, 6; Vol. II. 7, 8, 9; Vol. V. 4, 5.

W. Cunningham, *English Industry and Commerce*, 2, also 118, 128.

O. M. Dalton, *Byzantine Art*, 4, 5, 14.

F. Haverfield, *Romanization of Britain*, 2, 3.

C. E. Keyser, *Norman Tympana*, 7, also 36.

A. K. Porter, *Construction of Lombard Vaults*, 14.

For Chapters II to VIII.

Archaeologia, 1904, 63; 1914, 1915, 136.

H. Arnold, *Stained Glass*, 122, 137, 138.

J. Bilson, *The Beginnings of Gothic Architecture*, 31, 55.

P. Biver, *Bulletin Monumental*, 107, 115.

E. Blore, *Monumental Remains*, 115.

F. Bond, *Screens, Woodcarvings*, 130.

Camden Society, *Handbook of English Ecclesiology*, 73.

G. G. Coulton, *Medieval Garner*, 47, 65, 66, 76, 78.
„ *Social Life in Britain*, 76, 81, 120, 125.
F. H. Crossley, *English Church Monuments*, 115.
H. Druitt, *Costume in Brasses*, 107.
A. Gardner, *French Sculpture* (*Medici Portfolio*), 64, 79.
H. Hallam, *Middle Ages* (1868), 98.
A. Harvey, *Castles and Walled Towns of England*, 98.
W. H. St J. Hope, *Rochester Cathedral*, 30.
T. G. Jackson, *Renaissance Architecture*, 139.
A. Jessopp, *The Great Pillage*, 76, 129.
Jusserand, *English Wayfaring Life*, 126.
E. Lefèvre Pontalis, *Champagne Méridionale*, 82.
W. R. Lethaby, *Medieval Art*, 79, 90.
„ *Westminster Abbey and the King's Craftsmen*, 79, 83, 109, 121, 134.
E. Mâle, *L'Art Religieux du XIII siècle en France*, 77.
C. H. Moore, *Gothic Architecture*, 73.
W. Papworth, *R.I.B.A. Trans.* 1860—1861, 75.
J. T. Perry, *Dinanderie*, 28, 35.
E. K. Prideaux (Bishop), *Building of Exeter*, 133.
E. S. Prior, *Architectural Review*, 1906, 74.
„ *English Medieval Alabaster*, 134, 135.
G. G. Scott, *Gleanings from Westminster Abbey*, 82.
E. Sharpe, *Architectural Parallels*, 58.
A. P. Stanley, *Memorials of Westminster Abbey*, 83.
G. E. Street, *Gothic Architecture in Spain*, 76.
A. H. Thompson, *English Monasteries*, 26, 43, 122, 123.
„ *English Parish Churches*, 129.
„ *Exeter Fabric Rolls*, 87, 114.
H. Turner, *Domestic Architecture in England* (Parker), 74.
„ *Roxburghe Tracts*, 83, 95.

REFERENCES TO PLATE IV

CANTERBURY

A. Lanfranc's church 1065 (in outline).

B. Conrad's quire 1093.

B and C. New quire 1175.

C. Trinity chapel 1180.

Lanfranc's nave was rebuilt *c.* 1380—but the north-west tower remained—to be pulled down in 1834.

WINCHESTER

A. Walkelyn's church 1079 (East end in outline). Rebuilt 1107.

B. de Lucy's chapels 1195.

C. Quire rebuilt *c.* 1310.

D. Nave remodelled 1371—1400.

E. East chapel *c.* 1500.

The first church had a "narthex" or western hall of uncertain plan.

REFERENCES TO PLATE V

ELY

A. First church 1083—1130. Made cathedral in 1109.

B. Western Hall *c.* 1170.

C. Galilee *c.* 1200.

D. Chapels 1235—1250.

E. Lantern *c.* 1325.

F. Lady chapel *c.* 1330.

G. Quire rebuilt *c.* 1335.

DURHAM

A. Quire and Transepts 1093—1100.

B. Nave vaulted *c.* 1130.

C. Galilee *c.* 1170.

D. Nine Altars *c.* 1250.

The north porch and a great deal of outside work is now modern.

Plate II

MAP OF SITES
of pre-Conquest,
Anglo-Norman, and
Early Gothic building
illustrating the ancient dioceses
Lindisfarne
DURHAM
Ruthwell
Bewcastle
Tynemouth
Hexham
Lanercost
Carlisle
Escomb
Auckland
Durham
CARLISLE
Gosforth
Whitby
Easby
Rivaulx
Byland
Ripon
Fountains
Furness
Kirkstall
York
Selby
YORK
Roche Abbey
ST ASAPH
LICHFIELD
Lincoln
BANGOR
Southwell
Shrewsbury
Wenlock
LINCOLN
Lichfield
Norwich
Castor
Peterborough
NORWICH
Earls Barton
ELY
HEREFORD
WOR-CESTER
Brixworth
Paxton
Ely
ST DAVIDS
Northampton
Cambridge
St Edmundsbury
Worcester
Hadstock
Elstow
Strata Florida
Hereford
Tewkesbury
St Davids
Deerhurst
Stewkley
Colchester
Dore
Gloucester
Oxford
LONDON
Llanthony
Dinton
Iffley
St Albans
LLANDAFF
Waltham
Malmesbury
Reading
London
Llandaff
Langford
SALISBURY
Rochester
Bath
Bradford
ROCHR
Canterbury
WINCHESTER
CANTERBURY
Wells
Barfreston
Glastonbury
Salisbury
BATH & WELLS
Winchester
CHICHESTER
EXETER
Melbury Bubb
Romsey
Chichester
Lewes
Exeter

Plate III

SAXON IVORY
(Victoria and
Albert Museum)

CHAPTER I

THE BEGINNINGS, TO 1080

The great occasions of medieval art came to England, as to West Europe, in the crafts of church-building and church-decoration. With us the great building era came as the sequel of certain political events whose consummation in the Norman Conquest joined England to the Latin civilizations of West Europe. But English culture had already determined its quality in pre-Conquest church-building, and the Saxon ancestry of our artists, if in the background for a while, asserted itself in some two or three generations. Before the end of the twelfth century Anglo-Norman abbey-building was going otherwise than in Normandy, and in the thirteenth the English cathedral was of a different expression from the continental. We are justified therefore in dealing with our English story of art as one of interest in its special beginnings.

A. THE SAXON ARTS

(*a*) The Roman Occupation. (*b*) Mission-Culture from Rome. (*c*) Keltic Resurgences. (*d*) Anglian Sculpture. (*e*) Byzantine Art-Models. (*f*) Norse Culture and Carlovingian Art-Schools. (*g*) The Wessex Era. (*h*) Saxon Church-building. (*i*) Its Masonic Ineptitude.

(*a*) The Roman Occupation

Pre-Conquest art in England had its quality in the early evangelization of the British Isles, and obtained a high place in the monumental record of West Europe. The early Anglian crosses in Britain, and later the sculptured reliefs and "roods" of the South Saxons are notable for their figure-work. So too are the ivory carvings of the same school[1], and the Winchester manuscripts. The style adopts classic traditions, but is no child

[1] See opposite, also the author's *Med. Fig.-Sculp. in Eng.* pp. 136—142.

of the Roman occupation of Britain. In Italy, France, and Spain the direct classical lineage can be claimed—the arts derive from the Roman crafts, just as do the Romance tongues from Latin. But no such sequence was effective either for English speech or art. Not for the reason that Roman civilization had been less established, prosperous, or capable than in other parts of the Roman Empire. The Romans were in Britain for nearly 400 years—a stretch of time, say, from Henry VIII's reign to our day. The villas of the Roman agriculturists show how widely settled and prosperous was the community[1]. In the third century Britain had become a wealthy country, rich with the commerce of corn exports: we read that 800 vessels carried her harvests to the Roman cities of the Rhine[2]. But on the withdrawal of the Roman legions, the British shores were open to barbarian raids. The Saxons in some hundred years had wasted and depopulated all the chief areas of the Roman civilization and in the desolation of the cities had obliterated city life. There was lost to our island the Roman craft organization, that had been that of civic practice.

(*b*) Mission-Culture from Rome

Thus two centuries lie between the Roman culture—*imperial and pagan*—and the Neo-Roman—*papal and missionary*. In 597 came Christian art again to England brought by the official converters from Rome. Then in the seventh, eighth, and ninth centuries, as Saxons, Jutes and Anglians, and then the Danes, became settled and Christianized, their successive conversions make for three hundred years a period all through which Anglo-Saxon culture was expressed in ecclesiastic function. As such it has to be styled a branch of Carlovingian. But on the continent, the Carlovingian artist was in immediate touch with ancient craft tradition, and he was nearer too to the Eastern sources of ecclesiastic art. Moreover there survived abroad the

[1] F. Haverfield, *Romanization of Britain*, 1912, Chap. IV.

[2] W. Cunningham, *English Industry and Commerce*, 1910, pp. 54, 55.

civic organizations of culture, for in West Europe generally the Roman cities were taken as the capitals of religious authority. In England, however, the raiding centuries gulfed city life, and a tardy civilization had to grow up in agricultural homesteads. They are farmstead communities, those of associated cultivators that the "tons" and "hams" of our village names bear witness to. The Roman traditions of craft came as a *missionary*[1] gospel to a scattered population.

(*c*) Keltic Resurgences

The official conversion of a King's court in A.D. 598 was the direct outcome of Saint Augustine's mission from Rome, but it had no wide issue outside Kent. The South Saxons were still inhabitants of villages (*pagans*) seventy-five years after, when the Council of Whitby determined our church as Roman. The title page of English art is not to be seen at Canterbury at all, but was set up in Northumbria by Wilfrid's propaganda as part of the orthodox ecclesiastic polity that he carried determinately northward as Bishop of York, 670[2]. But during both sixth and seventh centuries there had been making back from Christian Ireland the reflex tides of Keltic Christianity; only as much as Wilfrid and Benedict Biscop put Rome upon Iona, English church art may be said to have been born as a Roman cult, in a population, diversely missionized but still largely pagan.

The Anglian monuments[3] of the late seventh century, that are the earliest substantial achievements of English art, have thus their three sides: (1) the *pagan* or village craftsmanship that had been markedly the metal-workers' dexterities of pattern: (2) the Keltic monk-culture that developed specially as a cross-worker's masoncraft: (3) the Roman ecclesiastic cult whose motives of figure-designing were the expression of manuscript drawing and ivory carving. We recognize the play of these elements in the

[1] Haverfield, *Rom. of Brit.* Chap. VIII. See also Baldwin Brown, *The Arts of Early England*, Vol. I. pp. 64, 65.

[2] *Op. cit.* pp. 173—176. [3] See Map of Sites, Pl. II.

Ormside Bowl[1], in the Lindisfarne "Gospels[2]," and particularly in the Anglian crosses[3]. In their ornaments Roman saints and Eastern vine-scrolls are seen mixed with Keltic bosses and interlacements.

(*d*) Anglian Sculpture

The figure-reliefs are upon the stone crosses at Bewcastle and at Ruthwell in Dumfries. But the Anglian style shown in these monuments must not be supposed the work of any single artist imported by Wilfrid. Northumbria in the seventh century extended far into Scotland, and throughout its area there are found Anglian crosses, in such numbers that their working implies a widespread craft necessarily native. Yet the sculptors clearly had access to patterns of the city craftsmanship of East Europe, as well as to those of the village life of the North. There are vine-scrolls and peacocks, doves pecking at grapes, and winged genii. Something of the same kind appears in the Carlovingian ornament generally, but the famous ivory chair of Maximian at Ravenna (considered to be the work of Alexandrian craftsmen) supplies, better than other known work of the early centuries, the analogues of both the figure-work and the vine-scrolls of our cross carvings[4]. There is record too of an architecture reminiscent of the East. Wilfrid built churches of note adorned with polished columns and images; so we read of them as existing at Hexham for some 500 years, and still exciting the admiration of the Augustinian Canons of the twelfth century, though the crypts ascribed to Wilfrid have now to our eyes little distinction of fine masoncraft[5].

[1] See illustration, Baldwin Brown, *op. cit.* Vol. v. Pls. XXX, XXXI.

[2] *Op. cit.* Vol. v. Pl. XXXIII.

[3] *Op. cit.* Pls. XII, XIV.

[4] See for illustration O. M. Dalton, *Byzantine Art*, pp. 203, 204, also T. G. Jackson, *Byzantine and Romanesque Architecture*, Vol. I. p. 158.

Baldwin Brown, *op. cit.* Vol. I. pp. 263 seq.

(*e*) Byzantine Art-Models

In the Anglian work of the seventh and eighth centuries we recognize how much West Europe owes to Byzantine civilization as handing on during the dark ages the subjects and processes of all craft-design[1]. One turns to Theodore of Tarsus, made Archbishop in 670, as not only the organizer of English churchmanship, but as art missionary too, and bringing into England, if not Greek workmen, at any rate, the immediate cult of Byzantine missals and ivories[2]. It has been customary to associate culture specially with Italy, and to speak of Christian art as necessarily derived from Rome. But we should realize how mixed and disconnected have been the workings of Mediterranean art in North Europe and how they have been objects more than artists that have carried Eastern ideas to the West. In the barbarous centuries Italy, too, was barbarous, so that for long Irish, rather than Roman, Christianity was the accepted beacon of northern culture—proselytizing Lindisfarne by Iona, sending missionaries to Gaul and even in the ninth century founding Keltic monasteries in Italy.

It was with art as with literature. Cuthbert of Lindisfarne and Bede of Jarrow brought Letters into North England but it was as a missionary gift, and moreover from two sources—from Ireland as well as from Rome. And if for Benedict Biscop and Wilfrid stonecraft was *mos Romanus* as a church-building, it had shape too in religious trophies, in crosses like those of Bewcastle and Acca, set up in the Keltic tradition of the standing stone[3]. So was it too with sculptured interlacements and painted miniatures like those of the Lindisfarne "Gospels[4]": Christian sculpture as a stone craftsmanship, and painting as a manuscript-

[1] Baldwin Brown, *op. cit.* Vol. v. pp. 284 seq.

[2] See O. M. Dalton, *Byz. Art*, pp. 236—237.

[3] See illustration in *Med. Fig.-Sculp. in Eng.* p. 110, also Baldwin Brown, *Arts of Early Eng.* Vol. v. Pl. XXV.

[4] *Op. cit.* Vol. v. Pl. XXXIII.

illumination, were imported to the British Isles, just as Buddhist art went as a religious craft to Ceylon and to Java: or as our missionaries to-day establish craft-schools: or when for the Propagation of the Gospel the wares of London church-furnishing firms are taken out to India.

(*f*) Norse Culture and Carlovingian Art-Schools

In the graftings of taste and design upon native arts, no head of missionary teaching develops. Survivals of ritual may last on, but no creative art tradition of continuing efficiency is induced. At any rate in Northumbria the Anglian figure-carving in a century or so was effete, and had degraded itself to the level of a South Sea Island zoomorphism[1].

Towards the end of the eighth century, however, a less artificial culture appeared. The ancestors of the Scandinavian hordes that were then descending upon England had maintained in their eastern homes an overland commerce with the East at the back of the Roman Empire. The pagan cults of Thor and Odin had developed themes of decoration, and motives of workmanship, founded on the stuffs and metal works of Greek design called Scythian, which seem responsible for Keltic pattern[2]. The West European dispersions of peoples explain how, with the Danish or Norse incursions, there came motives of Scandinavia into our culture. In the ninth and tenth centuries the Danes, who had harried and made desolate the Anglian mission-field, remained to establish townships and trading centres, in which the social crafts, discontinued since the Romans, grew into practice again. Christian building developed life and thought into art expression: but in that it did so, it derived from the eighth century culture of Charlemagne's imperial capital at Aix-la-Chapelle. Thus arose the second expression of pre-Conquest

[1] See example at Durham illustrated *Med. Fig.-Sculp. in Eng.* p. 102.

[2] Italian origin is now discounted. See Baldwin Brown, *Arts of Early England*, Vol. I. Ch. XVI.

civilization, racial and endemic in north and east, sporadic in south and west. The most striking of Viking monuments left are crosses, such as that of Gosforth[1], where appear, not the *Graeco-Roman* motives of Christian figure-subject, but those of the Norse pagan cults, with relief representations of animals and hunters. There is for example the base of such a cross, now in use upside down as a font at Melbury Bubb in Dorset[2]. For the conversion of the Scandinavian settlers was in the ninth century due to Irish Christianity as well as to monastic missionaries from the Rhine[3]. So we find an art of stonecraft joining hands with both Keltic and Carlovingian cultures yet in itself making the basis of a native expression. For in this second era of pre-Conquest art the Mid-England Christian had become a church-builder, and religious motive grew to expression in problems of construction. The planning of the Christian church had to develop under the economies of local conditions administered by native workmen. There were wrought versions of Carlovingian building with the characteristic "double-light" window, "pilaster strips" and "long and short" coigns[4]. But in the doorways of Mid-England churches there appears a typical Irish-Viking style of relief sculpture: thus it survived the Norman Conquest, laying a foundation of English work in the twelfth century[5].

(*g*) THE WESSEX ERA

The third era of pre-Conquest art was that which gave special expression to an English national church; and this was in the

[1] See for illustration *Med. Fig.-Sculp. in Eng.* pp. 115, 126.

[2] *Op. cit.* p. 126. Wessex culture was dosed rather than penetrated by Irish-Viking culture.

[3] Deerhurst and Brixworth, Baldwin Brown, *op. cit.* Vol. II. pp. 298 seq.

[4] See St Benedict, Cambridge; also Earls Barton, S. Gardner, Pl. XXI.

[5] *Med. Fig.-Sculp. in Eng.* pp. 152 seq. See also for a whole body of examples C. E. Keyser, *Norman Tympana*, 1905.

Wessex kingdom, when King Alfred's Peace of Wedmore 878 had given it security. The decadent Anglian masoncrafts of the north, and the Irish-Viking schools of the Danelaw were only slowly responsive to the South English culture. Still in the first years of the eleventh century Wessex art would seem to have had its monuments in England from Dorset to Yorkshire[1]. Its distinctive character developed in the peculiar ecclesiastic civilization, so that in the ninth-century monastic establishments of South England art went on parallel lines with the Othonian Renaissance[2]. It is to be noted that many of the Saxon foundations of monks and nuns were refounded after the Conquest: indeed illustration of Wessex style remains for the most part in connection with such at Romsey, Barking, and Winchester. The Danish overlording of Canute had small effect on these Saxon culture-crafts which to the middle of the eleventh century maintained their native distinction[3]. Not till 1060 did the Saxon complexion of our earliest Romanesque yield to Benedictine introductions, when the great abbey-building of the Normans had started West European art on a new career.

(*b*) SAXON CHURCH-BUILDING

The monuments of pre-Conquest architecture, as illustrating the sources of English culture, have come down to us in typical specimens. The Irish cell-church remains in a developed example at Escomb in Northumberland[4]: the expression of the Carlovingian mission-field is seen in the aisled plannings and the west towers of Deerhurst and Brixworth[5]: the national ecclesiastic type appears at Bradford-on-Avon[6]. The official church-building with its apsidal sanctuaries and passage crypts was by the side of the native a dying tradition[7]—Roman influence

[1] Examples are given *Med. Fig.-Sculp. in Eng.* pp. 131 seq.

[2] *Op. cit.* p. 165.

[3] *Op. cit.* pp. 132—144.

[4] See Baldwin Brown, *Arts of Early Eng.* Vol. II. pp. 110 seq.

[5] *Op. cit.* pp. 171, 299.

[6] See S. Gardner, Pl. I.

[7] See S. Gardner, Figs. 17, 21; Baldwin Brown, *op. cit.* Vol. II.

was persistent indeed but continually overlaid. English distinctions seem definitely established in the century and a half that immediately preceded the Norman Conquest, for the Keltic square-chambered, unaisled planning prevailed in spite of the Roman and Rhenish missionary[1]. The typical pre-Conquest church shows the oblong nave, with narrow entry to a square sanctuary, with no west door, but often porches[2] projecting north and south; and later with a lofty square, sheer tower opening from the west end of nave[3]. So were planned the churches by whose Saxon tradition was moulded thereafter English building.

(*i*) ITS MASONIC INEPTITUDE

There was however no lack of accomplishment or learning implied in Saxon refusal to build to models of continental church-design. As was Saxon literature, so was pre-Conquest building exhibiting itself as a craft in the hands of learned churchmen. But so it had the defects of its qualities: dictated by conscious design its architecture was a formula, not a creative practice; non-progressive because without experiment in construction, born of taste and draughtsmanship but divorced from the realities of a progressive industrial evolution. It retained for example the barbarian inefficiencies of monolithic or big-blocked construction. Its arches are turned with irregular ill-shaped voussoirs, or often are mere tracings in stone, the simulacra of building[4]. In its curious block-methods "pilaster strips" represent

pp. 116 seq. As to the cross-plan of pre-Conquest churches see pp. 306 seq. For the Cambridge reader there are examples at Paxton, near St Neots, and Hadstock near Linton of the latest Saxon types.

[1] *Op. cit.* Vol. II. pp. 304 seq.

[2] See T. G. Jackson, *Byzantine and Romanesque Arch.* pp. 193 seq.

[3] See St Benedict, Cambridge; also Oxford, S. Gardner, Fig. 39. See too Pls. XXI, XXXIII.

[4] Examples of Saxon methods are illustrated by S. Gardner, Fig. 16, Pls. XXXII, XXXIII. Bradford is shown Pl. I and Earls Barton Pl. XXI.

columns, and stone bandings project as "labels" outlining arches and pediments. In structural expression the Saxon building was inefficient, for just the reasons that much modern architecture is puerile, subordinating practical uses to stylistic design. On the other hand, the Saxon monasteries had painters who drew with an accomplished facility of cloister-craft in the tenth and eleventh centuries. The manuscripts of Winchester and St Albans have left us remarkable works of free figure-drawing, distinguished by their fineness as well as by the peculiar flutter of the draperies. The style is distinct and is in immediate connection with the composition with sensitive rendering of relief. For a hundred years after the Conquest no power or play of expression, such as the Saxon mason put into the Langford Rood[1] or the Bradford Angel[2], illuminated the works of the Anglo-Norman building-mason. The heads in the Chichester reliefs, representing the Raising of Lazarus[3], have the emotion and half-faced profile of Winchester drawings, of a quality unfathered on any Norman sculptor. So also the great Rood of Romsey Abbey[4] is Saxon and an insertion in the twelfth-century wall. There are other instances of similar preservations by the Norman builders, who themselves had no skill of an equal artistic sensitiveness: that the thirteenth-century sculpture and painting of English artists were to recover. But for a hundred years the building-mason was a mere carver of grotesques.

In this analysis of pre-Conquest art the distinctions of race have been considered unimportant, as compared with the evangelist introductions that ecclesiastics attempt. Viewed on the ground of racial aptitude for art, the English stock, whether as the Anglian of Northumbria, as Danish of Mercia, or as late Saxon of Wessex, claims monuments which, by the side of what remains abroad of the date, are conspicuous in number as well as in their quality. It cannot therefore be maintained that

[1] See author's *Med. Fig.-Sculp. in Eng.* p. 132. [2] *Op. cit.* p. 135.
[3] *Op. cit.* pp. 138—140. [4] *Op. cit.* p. 123.

the mixture of Saxon blood was in our island inimical to aesthetic capacity, or that English art had to wait for introduction from Normandy. The continental culture, that was initiated by the Conquest, was no racial transformation, but the opportunity of a great building art. For indeed the immense constructions of the Anglo-Norman abbeys were deficient in the quality of sympathetic expression which human life obtains in the graphic art of sculpture.

B. THE NORMAN ARTS

(*a*) Barbarous Italy and France. (*b*) Buildings—Byzantinesque and Romanesque. (*c*) Byzantine Figure-motives. (*d*) First Building of Churches. (*e*) Its Structural Energy—Local and Various. (*f*) Its Decorative Uniformity. (*g*) Its Economic Efficiency as Benedictine. (*h*) Its Constructional Expediency. (*i*) Introduction into England.

(*a*) Barbarous Italy and France

The European Romanesque was in origin and expression a craft of builders, and its sudden appearance in West Europe is one of the wonders of art history. For six centuries barbarisms had accumulated layer by layer: Goth, Visigoth, Lombard and Frank had deposited them. Now in the eleventh century an elemental force of creative craft-practice, breaking through the débris of the classic arts, like an intrusive lava consolidated itself with them. After the barbarians had swept Italy, Ravenna in the sixth century had succeeded to Rome as the capital of West Europe: yet the Ravenna building remains in evidence as a barbarous masonry with a decrepit science of arch-building[1]. Impotent had been classic tradition to preserve the ordinary capacities of masons' workmanship. As at Toscanella[2], so at other ninth and tenth century sites, at Torcello for example, the masonry is rough and barbarous. Not till A.D. 1000 under Byzantine tutelage, the skills of construction have revived at Venice,

[1] T. G. Jackson, *Byzantine and Romanesque Arch.* Vol. I. pp. 150 seq.

[2] *Op. cit.* p. 216.

Pisa and Milan sufficiently to make Italian building consequential to the history of European art.

Small were they in France to judge by the existing cathedral at Beauvais: where the early and late centuries are seen side by side, the Merovingian nave in all its puny incapacity of the ninth century, and the enormous quire of the master masons of the thirteenth. In some four hundred years was the art of architecture advancing step by step to this height of achievement. But it was not a decorative evolution, but constructional adventure. Architecture was remade by remaking the items of building, items long before invented, but grown stale in their academic senility. The classic uses of *column* and *architrave* existed as the prerogative of building, but becoming mere symbols of classic *style*, they lost constructional sense. Then in the fulness of time came the Romanesque building experiment: there was renewed the vitality of the orders, recreated as Pier, Arch, and Vault. As such they recovered the expression of *work*. They became *Gothic*—and what in the Christian basilica had been academic tradition, in the Gothic cathedral was a structural science, the assured economy of craftsmen who knew themselves capable for the calculated fabric of the medieval church.

(*b*) Buildings—Byzantinesque and Romanesque

It was towards the year 1000, in Lombardy in North Italy, that the experimental crafts of building succeeded to the covering in of areas with masoned vaults in bays. Such was the first step in the scientific construction of great churches[1]. But it was not for the Italian mason to discover the Gothic economies. In Italy in this same eleventh century, at St Mark's, Venice, and then at Pisa, Byzantinesque, as we may call the adapted science of the Eastern Empire, grew responsible for architecture: and this was a veneered construction, with schemes of decorative elegance that the Greek crafts applied to the domed church-

[1] See San Ambrogio, Milan, illustrated, *op. cit.* pp. 261—264.

building of the East[1]. By way of Italy the square *bay* of the Eastern domical church made its way into the experiment of the builders of West France[2]. But the arcaded aisle was alien to the domed plan; and so square bays in Lombardy, along the Rhine, in Provence and West France express southern conditions[3]. Lighted by small windows, they developed solemn caverned immensities; but masons' science was not advanced to Gothic economy. So little, that in the mid-thirteenth century the Romanesque of Germany, South France and the Mediterranean centres knew nothing of the skeleton construction that, in the planning of Gothic bays and the traceried elegance of Gothic windows, the masons of Picardy had perfected. The northern church-building had found its masonic economies in the piers and arches of the aisled basilica, because the northern builders had, for material, not concrete or marble but the freestones of West Europe; had to light their churches for northern skies, and roof them to withstand the rains and snows of the Atlantic terrain. In the physical and climatic conditions of North France and of England came the genius to create the specific sense of Gothic art.

(*c*) Byzantine Figure-motives

It was to a different issue that the decorative Byzantinesque of the East had set its endeavour—because in the mosaics and the paintings of domes and barrelled-vaults there were expressed the crafts of Christian symbolism. This was for the West as well as for the East, for Byzantine plaques, ivories, and metal

[1] See St Mark's, Venice, *op. cit.* p. 220 and Pisa, pp. 258 seq.

[2] See St Front, Périgueux, T. G. Jackson, *op. cit.* Vol. II. p. 34. The Romanesque, of Normandy and England, of Flanders, Picardy and Burgundy, was less a style than a condition of masoncraft advanced by experiment to the solution of the vault problem that the aisled basilica of the Roman plan set to constructors.

[3] See T. G. Jackson, *op. cit.* Vol. II. pp. 34 seq.

works were to be effectually contributive to the arts of Gothic painting and sculpture. By their use and in their service West European churches came into direct connection with the Christian magnificence of the Eastern church[1]. For the arts of pagan sculpture and painting were derelict. Figure-work of human flesh had been banned by Christianity as devilish both in East and West. Also it became distasteful to the Romanesque sense to use the tepid allegory of early Christian design, such as we see at Rome, or Arles[2]. The classic figure-treatment seems never to come into northern practice as of the Imperial Roman prescription. Only as passing through the meshes of Carlovingian or Irish-Viking zoography, and as having become less allegoric than magical—only as disguised as a Norse weird, were men and beasts to occupy the fabulist in the twelfth century (see forward pp. 35, 36).

(*d*) First Building of Churches

The halting steps which led building methods away from their classical notation were taken in Italy. In church-building the canons of Vitruvius could no longer be in force when a mixed lot of classical columns were re-used, or when in default of any columns at all, some method of pier-building had to take their place. There is little substance in the legend, that the Comacines, as a guild of traditionary masons in Como, were the inheritors of the craft collegia of Rome, passing on the secrets of masonry. It rests on inconclusive evidence as to the Lombard building of the eleventh century, and can claim no credence whatever for the evolution of northern Romanesque[3]. With Lombard ecclesiastics coming northward, there came plans and ideas for churches[4]. But craft cannot travel in a schoolman's

[1] O. M. Dalton, *Byz. Art*, pp. 80 seq.

[2] A Sarcophagus at Arles is figured, T. G. Jackson, *Byz. Rom. Arch.* Vol. I. p. 148.

[3] *Op. cit.* pp. 211 seq.

[4] A. K. Porter, *Lombard Vaults*. In Italy tenth-century building created bay-design in the exigency of church construction.

baggage. And indeed both in Italy and Normandy church construction disproves assumptions of Freemasonry. A total exhaustion of the Roman craft-formulae was the condition that was essential for the evolution of new building, because the exigences of the West European civilizations needed new constructions, not secret or privileged designs but the open experiments of masoncraft seeking new expression.

(*e*) Its Structural Energy—Local and Various

The stirring of the dry bones came in the energy of a new race. Whereas the ninth and tenth centuries had been those of the Viking inroads, in the field of their furies sprang up new arts of building. In Sicily and Lombardy as well as up the Rhine, all round the English coasts and along the west shores of France, the eleventh and twelfth centuries witnessed a great energy of architecture, as if bred in a generation or two wherever the Norse sea-king came into the ruling stock. Like Arab blood for horse-breeding, so would seem the Norman stock for architecture. And special demonstration of this Viking capacity was in North France, in the Dukedom of Normandy with its eleventh-century outburst of vigorous building—whose efficiency was transplanted by the Conquest into England and became there the nursery of the commanding experiments of Romanesque architecture. In 1040 was begun the Abbey of Jumièges, near Rouen, not only the largest erection of masonry that had been built in West Europe since the Romans, but the most consequential for the after development of the medieval arts. Its stonecraft expressed the power of the mason: for, in accomplishing the monastic behests of accommodation and magnificence, he was (*c.* 1100) to make possible the strides towards Gothic in the Anglo-Norman building of Durham. The main line of the architectural advances, for the hundred years after the Conquest, became immediately and nationally English. Other lines can, no doubt, be traced for the Romanesque evolution into Gothic—

by Ravenna say to Aix-la-Chapelle; and then by Germigny les Prés on the side of construction; and by St Martin's at Tours, on the side of church-plan, to St Hilaire, Poitiers[1]; so to the Angevin Gothic, to that of Champagne and the Île de France. Romanesque construction was in fact to be a wide-spreading genesis of artistic life in the building of churches. By the end of the eleventh century it was proceeding by experiment in all parts of West Europe and showing itself everywhere with the greatest diversity of masonic intention.

(*f*) Its Decorative Uniformity

But if Romanesque varies as to structure, the decorative treatments of that structure show a strange uniformity all through the Romanesque church-building of Europe. In the twelfth century almost identical zodiacal medallions were carved round doorways—as in Italy at Pavia[2], so in England at York, in Greece at Athens, in North Spain at Ripoll.

The uniformity of the ornamental and the diversity of the structural arts were significant reflections of European life and thought in the eleventh century—because both were the religious necessity. In the birth of medieval civilization the power of Romanesque art lay in the successive monastic dominations. The creed of Christendom dictated identical symbolisms throughout the whole area of orthodoxy, and sculpture came into being as no fanciful invention of decorative taste but as the need of the time. It was the decree of church-discipline obtaining its publication by means of the architectural surfaces. In the age when Letters meant little—for few could read, and still fewer write—the dogmatic teaching of the Church found itself committed to the art of the mason. Thus in its most perfunctory uses the Romanesque pattern was never a mere ornamental or Raphaelesque composition.

[1] See illustrations, T. G. Jackson, *op. cit.* Vol. II. pp. 15, 41, 43.

[2] See illustration, *op. cit.* Vol. I. p. 266; also S. Gardner, LXXII, LXXIII.

(*g*) Its Economic Efficiency as Benedictine

On the other hand it was equally of the ecclesiastic function of building, that it spoke in terms of constructive activity. As the materials varied, so were the varieties of pier and arch, of vault and ceiling—produced not as fancies of taste but in the expediencies of local economy. The Romanesque structure expressed life and thought, sometimes in an open square-chambered planning with massive piers, domed areas and broad arches—all concrete-built because the limestone plateaux of South France lacked freestone[1]. In other regions it was planned with shafted piers and masoned arches, because thick bedded stone was ready to hand, as on the Rhine[2], or in West France[3]. In the North it had long aisled halls as in Normandy and England, for if stone was abundant in the oolite districts of North-west Europe, it was of small bedding, whereas oaks grew to be cut in lengths for roofing. Accordingly in Normandy and England the aisled basilica, with high long nave some thirty feet wide, made the economic area[4]. The significance of it all was that the mason's building skill was using material for the working purpose of his art. By tradition of some centuries of churchmen the disposition of the church-plan itself, and the whole law of church ornament, were throughout Europe expressing an orthodox fixity. Masoncraft was but just from its cradle, and its growth to manhood came in a construction which best met the religious demand by providing the material areas of ecclesiastic ambition.

Thus the building of immense churches grew in the eleventh and twelfth centuries to be a requirement of medieval civilization, owing to the widespread Benedictine institution of monastic dignity. The thought of its time found speech in the monks' church—three or four times larger in area than anything that

[1] See St Front and Solignac, T. G. Jackson, *op. cit.* Vol. II. p. 41.

[2] See Worms, *op. cit.* Vol. II. p. 13.

[3] See St Hilaire, Poitiers, *op. cit.* Vol. II. p. 437.

[4] See plans facing pp. 32, 33.

European builders had attempted for 500 years. It was as a proclamation of religious privilege that in the Benedictine church the monks' choir is under the central tower; dignity of architecture being given internally and externally[1]. The whole complex of monastic building was set out with corresponding assertion of stately circumstance. It was as the courtyard of a palace that the cloistered court of the monks had its loggias—the ordered passage-ways to the conventual buildings, chapter-house, refectory and dormitory[2].

(*b*) Its Constructional Expediency

The mason had not only to enclose, but to cover from the weather; and not only to cover, but to keep safe from thieves and safe from fire-destruction. In A.D. 1000 the contents of a church were counted the most precious things in the world. The relics of saints were under the altars—offerings of every kind, gold, and silver and works of art adorned the sanctuaries. A church was a treasure-house for religion, to be walled in and protected as is an arsenal for war. But if such conditions had equal urgency throughout Europe wherever churches were building, yet as compared with his southern brethren the builder of the North was faced by special problems, in that the dull northern skies made impossible the insignificant lighting that South Europe found convenient. For example in South France and Lombardy window openings were not wanted under the church vault[3]: but at Jumièges and Caen abbeys have the lofty *clerestory* whose name suggests its purpose, all along the nave[4]. In South Europe roofs are flat; wood was not available, nor its crafts practised for the purpose of church-building. But the oak forests and the Norse craftsmanship gave to northern

[1] See the lantern at Tewkesbury, S. Gardner, Pl. XXIV.

[2] See for English church-plans the author's *Gothic Art in Eng.* pp. 59—65.

[3] See for illustration T. G. Jackson, *op. cit.* San Ambrogio, Milan, Vol. I. p. 264; Le Puy, Vol. II. p. 44.

[4] Illustrated in Francis Bond, *Gothic Architecture in England*, pp. 320 seq.

builders the practical habit of erecting steep roofs over their ceilings, and so making them safe from snow[1]. Such factors of building economy led the Anglo-Norman masons onward step by step to the constructional enterprise of the great abbey-church. Its art came by experiment till it could build the high vault of Durham, stone-ceiled and *lighted* all along underneath its high ceiling. And the stupendous discovery for the art of architecture was, that it should do this by the science of masonry, shaping small stones into the coherence of an almost conscious stability[2].

(*i*) Introduction into England

So in the coming of the Benedictine civilization the barbaric inefficiency of a missionary tradition passed away: England acquired the energies of monastic architecture. There was a direct importation of Norman masoncraft for the years 1060—1070 in the immediate building of the Conquest—represented now in few material monuments—principally in the two fortresses, in the Castle now the University at Durham, and the Tower of London. The original chapels of both castles remain to illustrate the constructive energy and decorative savagery that were qualities of the Norman masons[3]. Only a conjectured plan and a few capitals survive of the Confessor's church at Westminster, 1064, the building of which is recorded as that of Norman Benedictines[4]. One valuable example in existence a hundred years ago was Lanfranc's tower at Canterbury, built *c.* 1070, but pulled down by "restorers" in 1840. The essential quality of the Norman Conquest was to appear in the settings out of the great abbeys, St Edmundsbury, 1070, St Albans, 1077, Winchester and Ely, 1081 (plans opp. pp. 32, 33).

[1] See S. Gardner, Pls. II, III and Pl. XXXV.

[2] Author's *Rome to Renaissance* will trace the evolution of Romanesque structure in Europe.

[3] See for Durham and Westminster capitals the author's *Med. Fig.-Sculp. in Eng.* pp. 147, 162.

[4] By William of Malmesbury, see T. G. Jackson, *Byz. Rom. Arch.* Vol. II. pp. 206 seq.

To sum up, the Norman Conquest was no bringing in of *artists* into England, nor was it, as had been the Anglian and Carlovingian cultures, a missionary craft-schooling. Its first effect was destructive of the distinctive Saxon culture, that had been of the church and studio rather than of the builder's yard. But by the clearance room was left for the Benedictine art of great abbey-building whose energetic expression will be described in the next chapter.

Viewed socially the architecture of the Norman Conquerors was of initial consequence to English style as in its ecclesiastical, so in its secular ambitions. The Conqueror did not allow the estates which he granted to develop into counties or dukedoms, and his underlords did not control country-sides, establish fiefs, and come into rivalry with the central authority. Castles were in England expressions of state defence, not strongholds of political assertion. Thus castellated architecture became domestic and manorial in England—it did not grow on into the palace. But this meant the greater distinction for the English churches. The Norman policy in respect of religious houses was to replace the loose Saxon rules by the disciplined institutions of continental monasticism. The new Benedictine foundations were made wealthy and powerful as buttresses of the Norman power[1]. They were established as frontier garrisons: at Durham, Chester or Gloucester they took up the defence of borders in strategical positions: at Ely and Norwich they dominated the last resistances of the Saxon population. And, moreover, in not a few cases the monks' church was made the Bishop's, an essential distinction for the English abbey-building. Though built for monks, it was the capitular church of his see, for the Bishop was Abbot. By the wealth and influence of the English Benedictines Anglo-Norman Romanesque held its position for some fifty years as foremost in the European evolution of architecture.

[1] See the author's *Cathedral Builders*, pp. 30 seq. The Cathedrals of Durham, Ely, Norwich and Canterbury remain as conspicuous examples of the English Monastic Cathedral of the twelfth century.

CHAPTER II

MONASTIC ARCHITECTURE, 1080—1140

C. THE PLANNING AND THE BUILDING

(*a*) The Benedictine Church. (*b*) The Monastic Quire and Lantern. (*c*) The Nave. (*d*) The Great Cloister. (*e*) Shrine Extensions. (*f*) Abbey-Churches in Evidence. (*g*) Monastic Ateliers. (*h*) Vast Constructions. (*i*) Ecclesiastic Schooling. (*k*) The Triumph of Masoncraft.

(*a*) The Benedictine Church

The ancient churches of England, as we see them in service now, are mostly of two classes: (1) *cathedral* churches—large conspicuous buildings served by a special appointment of Dean, Canons, and other cathedral clergy, each the seat of a Bishop and the chief church of his *see*, held by him in the name of the state; (2) *parish* churches locally served by the rectors, vicars and curates, reckoned as the property of the parish, and used for its services. A third class of ancient church also remains, chiefly at Oxford and Cambridge as the chapels of colleges. Attached to private or corporate property these are served by a private appointment of clergy. In comparison with *cathedral* and *parish* churches private chapels are now a small matter. Yet they made the most important and consequential architecture of the Middle Ages. For the religious order had its churches outside any obligation to the community: it built and used them as private property. So since what we study as the important medieval monuments were, in their first buildings, not designed for public use, their architecture was not in that first instance of the *people* —but of the Benedictine institution that built it. It was because medieval culture developed in monasticism, because vast building-enterprises were the symbols of its operation, that the arts of church-building became instruments of a new art era in the world's history.

The debt that European civilization owes to the monks has generally been honoured by the historian. But the following summary of their social importance in England by B. Disraeli in his novel of *Sybil*, can be quoted: "They were proprietors that were never absentee—they spent their revenue in their estates; their churches were cathedrals, their schools colleges, their halls and libraries the muniment rooms of the kingdom; their woods, their waters, their farms, their gardens were disposed and managed on a scale and in a spirit, that made the country beautiful and the people proud of their country."

Moreover, for the five centuries of medieval architecture, these churches of the Benedictines in England out-classed in size and magnificence those of other institutions. Of less dignity was the secular church, *cathedral* or *parish*, that in the technical language of the Middle Ages was in the world, not cut off from it as was the church of regular monks and canons. When in the sixteenth century the monastic institution in England was dissolved, and its properties were confiscated, the monks' church lost its office. Abbeys and priories stripped and dilapidated, fell into ruin—many were razed off the face of the earth, many were appropriated in one way or other to *secular* use. Some of the most important such as Peterborough and St Albans have since the Dissolution become our cathedrals. Indeed for the study of the art-expression of medieval building that of English Cathedrals must be reckoned as of the monastic complexion.

(*b*) The Monastic Quire and Lantern

Many of the most conspicuous had been cathedral by the Conqueror's constitution: let us enter one of them, say by the west door at Norwich[1] or by the north porch at Durham[2]: the great hall of a palace opens to us, with massive piers, and bay beyond bay of arched solidity. We look upwards to an ordering of

[1] See Le Keux's engraving in the author's *Cath. Build.* Pl. 2.

[2] See F. Bond, *English Church Architecture*, p. 746.

the walls in stories[1]—to the arcaded openings of the triforium galleries that served monastic uses—to the *clerestory* letting in broad areas of light beneath the arching ribs of the monastic vault[2]. For in this construction of abbey-church building lay the state and circumstance of the Benedictine constitution[3]. We note piers composed of shafts which run from floor to ceiling in detailed ceremonious provision for a ceiling in specified bays. It is an ordered arrangement that, in its plenitude of massive masoncraft, speaks of immense resources and the power of a settled polity. At St Albans, Waltham, Ely, Durham, Norwich and Peterborough are abbey-churches of the Anglo-Norman development of architecture still in witness. At St Albans[4], Gloucester[5], or Norwich[6], the vista of the nave is seen still closed by the wall-like screen that shuts off the inner hall of the monastic quire. Behind this are now the stalls of the cathedral body; but the wall is that of the exclusive barrier which the ancient seclusion of a private service demanded. It was the Benedictine dignity that a thousand years ago fenced itself in behind this closed barrier.

The substantial intention of an architectural dignity is to be seen, too, in many of our great churches in the *lantern* of the crossing, the central expression—tower outside[7], inside an area of lighted space. North and south of it transepts with their chapels open out, conspicuous externally as projecting halls[8], and eastward we look up the long chancel to the apsidal ring of radiating arches indicating the chapel recesses[9]. If the forms

[1] S. Gardner, Pl. XXXVII.

[2] T. G. Jackson, *Byz. Rom. Arch.* Vol. II. pp. 225—226.

[3] For Waltham Abbey see S. Gardner, Pl. XXXV, for Peterborough Pl. LXXXVI.

[4] See F. Bond, *Goth. Arch. in Eng.* p. 14.

[5] *Op. cit.* p. 26.

[6] See the author's *Cath. Build.* p. 12.

[7] See Tewkesbury, S. Gardner, Pl. XXIV.

[8] See Winchester, Pl. XXXVI: also plans given here opposite pp. 32, 33.

[9] See Norwich, Pl. XLI.

of architecture are ever expressive such building has declared its purpose—the abbey-church was to be the house of a magnificent ritual, "occult, withheld, untrod." In it was the Sacred Shrine, the monastic possession of which consummated the theory of Benedictine civilization.

(*c*) The Nave

Now in England this Benedictine church was, as has been said, often made cathedral, and accordingly we see it as the great church of the diocese. The original massive stateliness may have yielded to later refinements in the quires of Canterbury, Ely, St Albans and Gloucester—in the last Gothic century as at Winchester, Canterbury and Ripon, the monastic naves have been built in a later mentality of art—yet inside and outside the set out of the Anglo-Norman architecture makes the overpowering impression to our eyes. It is what the Benedictine rule and the political necessity of the Norman Conquest cradled. The long English nave, the long English quire, and the wide stretch of English transept centring on the lantern, constitute the English church to the end of the Gothic story. But while the *chevet* of the continental church and its cliff-like façade with caverned porches were elaborated in Continental style, they were not in the English—because the circumstances of the Conquest made great church-building in England not civic, not episcopal nor political, but monastic[1].

Other details of this same expression of Anglo-Norman building may be briefly noticed. The necessities of conventual life have conditioned the English plan in the positions of *cloister*, *chapter-house*, *dormitory*, *refectory*, etc. The many bays of nave allowed full accommodation for these stately buildings, on the north or the south side according as the lie of the ground

[1] French cathedrals can be seen in T. G. Jackson's *Goth. Arch.* Reims, Vol. I. p. 111, Amiens, p. 123. For Canterbury see the author's *Cath. Build.* Pl. I, also for the whole comparison *Goth. Art in Eng.* pp. 78—82.

made convenient. The Benedictine arrangement was uniform throughout Europe as the settled ceremonial ordering of a vast organization: but some peculiarities attend the English use. The main public entrance to a continental church was normally at the west, and its twin-towered façade was symptomatic of continental design[1]. The architectural prestige of the Gothic cathedral as built in the Île de France made the towered front of the west end generally characteristic of Gothic building abroad. But not so in England, and the point has a traditional significance. The first church we read of, that of St Augustine, at Canterbury, was built with entrance on the south side[2], and side porches reappear in the Anglo-Norman abbey-churches, the main entrances being on the side of the nave unoccupied by the cloister—on the north side at Durham[3] and on the south at Canterbury[3] as rebuilt after the Conquest[4].

(*d*) The Great Cloister

On the *cloister* side of the English monastic nave[5] two entrance doorways from the loggia were elaborately decorated. The east alley in immediate connection with the chapter-house and dormitory was specially the state corridor of entrance, by which the monks passed into the quire of the church[6]. In the other alleys, from which opened the other door, were placed the library and *scriptorium* (writing room) of the monks, and also

[1] See Caen, F. Bond, *Eng. Ch. Arch.* p. 567.

[2] Willis's plan is given in T. G. Jackson, *Byz. Rom. Arch.* Vol. II. p. 211.

[3] See F. Bond, *Goth. Arch. in Eng.* p. 149.

[4] In many of our churches were spacious halls at the west end, as the Galilee at Durham, illustrated T. G. Jackson, *op. cit.* Vol. II. p. 227. There was a remarkably long "narthex" or entrance hall to the great Benedictine abbey-church of Winchester. At Peterborough and Ely the Porch-hall was planned transversely across the front and this west transept is specially English. (Plans opposite pp. 32, 32.)

[5] See plans, F. Bond, *Goth. Arch. in Eng.* pp. 148 seq.

[6] Ely doorway, T. G. Jackson, *op. cit.* Vol. II. p. 252.

the *lavatory* at which they washed their hands after dinner. Along the west side was the cellarer's, or steward's office, while the alley on the remaining side admitted directly to the refectory and to the offices in connection[1]. These details are mentioned because in England they had a development outside the monastic economy. It was a peculiar monastic imprint on English art that secular churches borrowed conventual appurtenances. The state cloisters and chapter-house of Lincoln and Salisbury are indications that the palace architecture of the first Benedictine ambition set a model of state for English cathedrals to follow (see on pp. 84, 85 below). Moreover its scheme of loggias, with the disposition of the rooms round them, was an introduction into North Europe of the Mediterranean house-plan.

(*e*) Shrine Extensions

Another way in which Benedictine building asserted itself was in the importance and development of shrine architecture in England. The crypt of the Saxon tradition expressed the cult of martyr-worship, derived from Roman evangelization. With a spacious undercroft were Anglo-Norman rebuildings at Worcester[2], Winchester[3] and Canterbury[4] in the extension of quires of the English Benedictines. In the twelfth century as the glory of shrines grew to greater circumstance, when the saints' relics were no longer left to be exhibited under the altar, but were housed on the level of the church floor behind it—this made occasion for that still further lengthening of the English church fabric which stretched it for Becket's shrine beyond the monks' quire at Canterbury, or for St Swithin's at Winchester. At Canterbury this persistent extension eastward made a church-length nearly double that of Notre Dame, Paris. Similarly

[1] A. H. Thompson, *English Monasteries*, p. 40.
[2] See S. Gardner, Pl. CVIII.
[3] See T. G. Jackson, *Byz. Rom. Arch.* Vol. II. p. 219.
[4] *Op. cit.* Vol. II. p. 213, also S. Gardner, Pl. XXXIX.

English abbey-churches, at Bury, at St Albans, and finally at Winchester and Canterbury, were longer than continental abbey-churches of their date[1].

(*f*) Abbey-Churches in Evidence

Such are some of the material indications that the Conquest by grafting the great resources of Benedictine civilization on to the tradition of Saxon art, gave the English a scheme of church-building that proceeded on different lines from the continental Romanesque. Its greater mass and more extensive ground-plan distinguish it at Winchester, St Albans, Durham, St Edmundsbury, Bath, Ely, and Norwich, to be named out of some forty or fifty monastic churches built in the fifty years after the Conquest[2]. They were carried to completion before 1140 and till the Dissolution remained in evidence without material enlargement. In their fabric arch construction, that had been hardly ventured on by the Saxon masons of 1050, was developed in a succession of daring experiments. At Ely in 1085[3] the setting out of the piers can be seen to propose a great achievement of masonry in the throwing of arches over the wide nave at some eighty feet from the floor-level. Though in this case not carried out, the disposition is that of an ordered scheme, conceived in the masonic forethought of master builders. Yet in the estimate of this art we must assign its generous skills to the conditions of the eleventh century, and not to mere workmen's practice.

It must be recollected that the Benedictine head of a monastic house was concerned in construction in a more direct way than

[1] The church at Cluny by the extension of its quire became the largest in Europe at the end of the twelfth century. See plan, F. Bond, *Goth. Arch. in Eng.* p. 150.

[2] Plans opposite pp. 32, 33; see also S. Gardner, Pls. XXXIV, XLI, for St Albans and Norwich.

[3] For illustration see F. Bond, *Eng. Ch. Arch.* p. 573.

as an onlooker on a system of building, or as a modern client who gets a design from an architect. The missionary tradition had attached the initiative and personal instruction in all the practical arts to the cleric. Thus to an Abbot like Lanfranc of Caen, or Gundulf of Rochester it was natural to act as the foreman-architect of his church-building. For in the eleventh and twelfth centuries monasteries were workshops of the working arts, so that the furnishings of an abbey-church, *c.* 1100—its shrines and altars, its hangings and its service books, its candlesticks and vestments were works of religious service in the life to which the monk had devoted himself.

(*g*) Monastic Ateliers

Moreover the building works had other offices besides the mere provision of church-space and its accessories. In the fabric itself was the standing school of theology and the library of medieval science. The churches were the consulted authorities, tables in stone of Christian Law. Imagery (*imagines*), with the graphic force of sculpture and painting, were part and parcel of the great church, as necessary to it as was the science of its stone bonding, or the disposition of its lighting. In its arts the monastic institution could do without the professional and commercial middleman who is the modern administrator. The Abbot's knowledge of building or of decorative art was practical, and his intentions of design and craft were immediately those of the *artifex*. Indeed the monk might, as often as not, be the craftsman himself, as the Abbot of Abingdon, named as a wonderful worker in gold and silver[1]. Not that every Bishop was a builder's foreman, or every Abbot a metal-worker or painter, but building, metal work, and painting were immediate expressions of monastic life and thought. All culture and all its inventive experiment were

[1] In A.D. 1050. See author's *Med. Fig.-Sculp. in Eng.* p. 93; also the Gloucester candlestick, p. 166. As to St Eloy, Bishop of Noyon, *c.* 650, see *Archaeologia*, 1914, 1915, pp. 124 seq., and for the bronze font at Liège see J. Tavernor Perry, *Dinanderie*.

of ecclesiastic craft, in the eleventh and twelfth centuries: in England our greatest churches, that now we have as cathedrals, were in their craft and in their art the assertion of Benedictine civilization.

(*b*) Vast Constructions

In some eighty years from 1040 the Romanesque masons of the north of Europe gave stone-work the capacity to advance on to Gothic, and this specially in Anglo-Norman church-building, with its immense ambitions of bulk and area, its lordly privilege of exclusion and palatial dignity, its appropriation of shrine sanctity and sacerdotal privilege[1]. The shrines of St Cuthbert at Durham and St Becket at Canterbury became the treasure-houses of a vast wealth: the Benedictine establishments of the twelfth century were outbidding the resources and credits of a monarchic or state taxation. But the vital force modelling English art in the generation of *c.* 1100 was the executive craftsmanship of English church-builders. Considering the area and population of the districts in which the English abbey-churches were distributed, the bulk of fabric in progress, say *c.* 1100, is amazing. Such was its substance that it has defied in many of our churches all the subsequent efforts of reconstruction or removal[2]. In many districts "Norman" architecture, as we call it, makes church-structures to this day. The ordinary proportions of the building crafts in a community could not have supplied sufficient artisans: there were needed all the able-bodied as in a war conscription. But with unskilled operators, Benedictine building had to simplify methods of masoncraft—as we see them, say, at St Albans[3], or at Colchester[4], in the first great abbey-structures. A building art

[1] See the Durham Sanctuary knocker, author's *Med. Fig.-Sculp. in Eng.* p. 169.

[2] See S. Gardner, Pls. XXXVII, XXXVIII, XL for examples.

[3] *Op. cit.* Pl. XXXIV. Also F. Bond, *Goth. Arch. in Eng.* p. 14.

[4] Both the Benedictine and Augustinian abbeys. See S. Gardner, Fig. 4.

of this wholesale kind could only be that of a craft of wallers, *coementarii*—concrete or mortar builders—with the smallest use of the stone-cutters[1]. The chiselling of stone is minimized to the utmost at Winchester, Gloucester and Tewkesbury in early work. Wall stones are roughly hammered to shape as if the craft of the Caen-stone masons from Normandy had been superseded. We see a concrete construction, rubble-faced, square angled; with piers often built as simple cylindrical drums of roughly coarsed masonry; with arches cut square or with coarse curvatures such as a tyro could dress with little apprenticeship[2].

(*i*) Ecclesiastic Schooling

Yet this coarsely built masonry was contemporary with the finished marble dexterities of St Mark's, Venice, or the Duomo of Pisa. Its significance is that in the enterprises of the great English abbey-builders an unskilled population, lay or serf, was being trained in the mysteries of masoncraft. Under similar circumstances a Bishop in a savage see might teach his native congregations to build the churches of his diocese. As indeed, after a hurricane that some years ago swept away every church in the Bahamas, an energetic and capable priest built, as the sole white among a population of negro descent; devised the dressing and laying of coral blocks with his own hands, and taught how churches might be hurricane proof. In such fashion, and so energized, was Gundulf's tower at Rochester built 1080[3].

Now in the church-building of the eleventh century massive rubble-built walls, seven or eight feet thick, meant a new art of construction: immediately preceding there had been the refined,

[1] In the assize of London 1212, stone-dressers are called *Sculptores lapidum liberorum*.

[2] See S. Gardner, Pls. XXXIV—XXXVI. See also Elstow, T. G. Jackson, *Rom. Byz. Arch.* Vol. II. p. 230.

[3] Pulled down in 1790. See W. H. St J. Hope, *Monograph on Rochester Cathedral*.

neatly fitted masonry of the Saxons, often elegantly chiselled but inefficient in a structural sense (see back p. 9). Accordingly these vast enterprises, in their apprenticeship of the Anglo-Norman population to church-building, brought into England the elemental force of creative art that the Saxon mason had lacked. Immediately that the constructive needs, the real begetters of art, discovered the ambition of progress, it was to be but a few years when the rough workers of the Winchester transept were succeeded by the stone-dressers of Durham quire. Great ambitions of building were found in Bishop Flambard who was successively Bishop of Winchester and Bishop of Durham,—concerned with the Christchurch Priory in Hampshire and then with the Durham Cathedral. Under his ecclesiastic direction we see the stone-cutter advancing the whole craft of masonry, so that it is no longer the rubble and concrete execution of the earlier abbeys. In them weight and mass were making, as they had made in Roman construction, the expediencies of the wall: at Durham now each individual stone has, by being shaped and dressed to a purpose, become part of an active scheme and in this has obtained the sense of economic efficiency[1].

(*k*) The Triumph of Masoncraft

To explain this let us look at Ely and Peterborough[2]: in their aisles the arcadings of the wall and the vault ribs of the ceiling are economies of masoncraft: stone is put together in shaped sculpture not as a formless conglomerate: the cutting mason has made each piece to a purpose. And by these economies resulted a wonderful achievement at Durham, the hanging of a stone cover of massive masonry eighty feet above the pavement[3], as far as we know, the first complete solution of the

[1] For Durham, S. Gardner, Pl. XXXVI; for Christchurch, T. G. Jackson, *op. cit.* Vol. II. p. 234.

[2] See F. Bond, *Goth. Arch. in Eng.* pp. 306, 315.

[3] *Op. cit.* p. 8. The high vaults of both quire and transept are accounted as built by 1099. J. Bilson, *Beg. Goth. Arch.* p. 261.

problem, by which the whole area of a church could be ceiled in a way that preserved the interior in the case of roof-conflagration. It allowed an outer roof to take off the water, keeping the fabric from decay; and as the crowning accomplishment it gave church interiors a direct lighting of broad windowings under the stone ceilings. Not only has stone chiselling so become expert, but the mechanics of church-building have discovered that they could, by use of little pieces of shaped stone, lift the vault to the height of the main ceiling of a great nave.

Both north and south the stone covering of a high nave had been the aim of Romanesque experiment, but the southern masonries of Lombardy[1], of the Rhine[2], or of Provence[3] had made for darkness instead of light. Durham nave has a clear lighting along its clerestory, and to effect this practical purpose the thrusts—that represent the energy of gravity in building—are scientifically regulated to bear on fixed points, and so are coupled to the ground in a chain of static equilibrium, for which science of pointed arch and flying buttress has come into use at Durham[4].

The centuries of Gothic building that were to follow, found expression in no other creed than that promulgated by Bishop Flambard's *ingeniator* (as the records call him) to save stone by workmanship. Some ten or twelve years of the experimental art of Durham blended use and execution in one purpose of design,—not as any fancy of effect dictated by taste, but as a working expediency of church-builders by whose skill the conditions of the Benedictine socialism were to be expressed.

[1] Illustrated, T. G. Jackson, *op. cit.* Vol. I. p. 264.

[2] *Op. cit.* Vol. II. p. 16.

[3] *Op. cit.* Vol. II. pp. 36, 44.

[4] See the arches under the roofs of the aisles: F. Bond, *Eng. Ch. Arch.* pp. 402, 403.

Plate IV

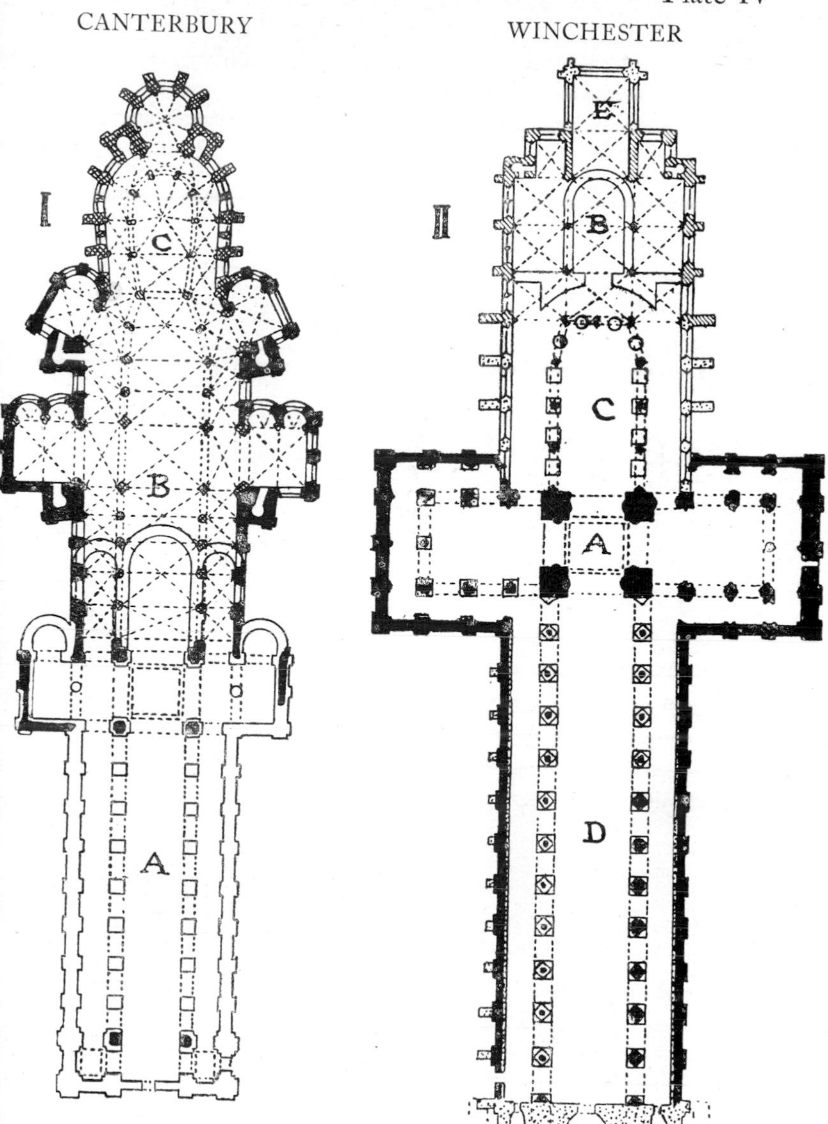

For references see p. xii

Plate V

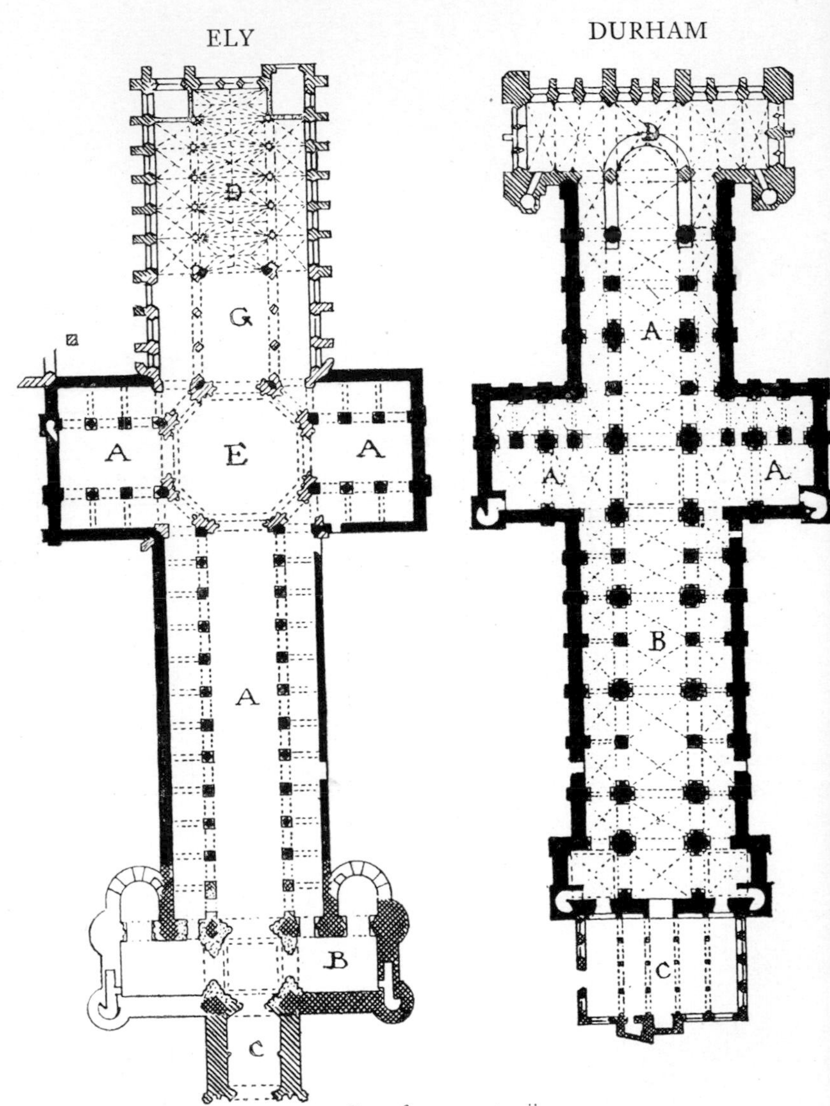

For references see p. xii

D. ROMANESQUE DECORATION

(*a*) Painted Wall-surfaces. (*b*) Sculptural Rudeness. (*c*) Cross Technique and Metal Work. (*d*) Tympanum Sculpture. (*e*) Manuscript Motives.

(*a*) Painted Wall-surfaces

Twelfth-century workmanship grew also as prompt to discover its genius in those exhibitions of craft which we entitle *decorative*—as specially works of sculpture and painting—the latter first, because of its immediate dependence on the conditions of the Benedictine building. The broad stretches of rubble-concrete or roughly hammered wall-stone, laid in with thick beds of mortar, the joints two inches thick, were skinned over with a thin plaster, on which the painter, the ecclesiastic trained in the craft-schools of the monastery, traced representations of the Saints[1]. To our eyes the stripped walls of the first Anglo-Norman churches seem examples of rude stonework, but this is a misinterpretation of their Romanesque intention. The finished surface of a Benedictine church, where it has come down to us intact, has had no tolerance for rough building textures. The contemporaneous churches in Italy to this day show their permanent decorations of mosaic and painting. The same graphic intention once made the walls of English churches[2] profuse of colour and pictorial design. Remains of painting abound: a well preserved example is in the crypt at Canterbury, where a recess in St Gabriel's chapel that had remained built up for many centuries was uncovered fifty years ago. It represents St Paul's shipwreck and is a distemper painting with considerable proficiency of draughtsmanship used broadly and with solid colour. The technique and motives of its display are as expert as in the splendid illuminated manuscripts of the twelfth century, such as the Winchester Bible. But it must be remembered that medieval art was practical, that is to say

[1] S. Gardner, Pl. XXIV; also see F. Bond, *Goth. Arch. in Eng.* p. 14.

[2] At Copford much restored, S. Gardner, Pl. CLXV.

it acknowledged its conditions whether on a page of MS. or on a wall-surface. The Romanesque wall painting is not a manuscript-illumination, but rather a declamation or piece of oratory offered us in colour—but specially speaking to the purpose of the massive architecture it adorns. The church-painting in Anglo-Norman art kept strictly to its themes as literature of its age, and so expressed the unbounded Benedictine mission for civilization in England, as in Europe generally.

(*b*) Sculptural Rudeness

When, however, from painting arts we turn to sculptural, we make another estimate of the first Anglo-Norman capacity. The expressive delicacy of the latest Saxon relief-work, as it is found in the great crucifixion at Romsey, may possibly be of a date after the Conquest[1]. The Saxon nunneries in Wessex, Romsey, Shaftesbury, Amesbury and Wilton, surviving the Conquest, seem to have had to hand Saxon craftsmanships with a sculptural capacity beyond what the Norman masons could supply. For if we look at the stoneworks that can be identified as specially Norman of the Conquest—for example at Durham Castle—their carvings are barbarous[2].

Moreover the great Anglo-Norman abbey-building of 1100, at St Albans, Winchester, Colchester, or Ely, has left us no sculpture: piers with their capitals and arches are laid out broadly and smoothly to give fields for painting[3]. Occasionally a head or some small piece of figure-work is seen carved in savage style, as is the case, too, with contemporary work in Normandy. Stone as building, not as sculpture, exercised the Norman capacity. Yet the English masons were in a generation or so to make such play with the motives derived from the Byzantine models that in executive skill and power of expression, English work was certainly on the same plane of sculptural achievement

[1] See author's *Med. Fig.-Sculp. in Eng.* pp. 134 seq. [2] *Ibia.* p. 147.

[3] St Albans is the best example, S. Gardner, Pl. XXXIV.

as any in Europe[1]. Indeed there was a foundation for the craft of relief-sculpture in England that was lacking elsewhere.

(*c*) CROSS TECHNIQUE AND METAL WORK

To understand this we must go back to Irish-Viking art. The relief-sculpture of the crosses, which are found all over the West of England, has its pattern outlines of subject in flat low relief with blunt edges—what was in fact a translation into stone of the flat wood carving of the Vikings[2]. This technique appears in some pieces that seem of the Saxon craft[3] of sculpture although built into Anglo-Norman work,—the figuring having been considered of value by the ornamentalist masons of the twelfth century. In the round, also, the technique of a wood carver appears in the label-heads of some of the Anglo-Norman buildings and in the grotesque heads of corbel-tables, which seem a translation of the projecting ends of wood timbers[4]. But also the metal crafts of the Benedictine cloister, of which we have documentary evidence as existing in England before the Conquest, may be brought into the question. Under the German Emperors of the eleventh century there were especially developed the arts of the ecclesiastical metal-workers, and in England we have examples of monk-craftsmen in metal[5], as well as in ivory.

(*d*) TYMPANUM SCULPTURE

But the English renaissance of the Irish-Viking sculptor is the remarkable episode that explains our medieval art of sculpture. The twelfth-century doorhead, or as it is called *tympanum*,

1 See author's *Med. Fig.-Sculp. in Eng.* pp. 149 seq.

2 Ibid. *op. cit.* pp. 126, 129.

3 As at Southwell, *op. cit.* p. 129, and in the Wenlock chapter-house.

4 As at Kilpeck, *op. cit.* p. 170.

5 See the Gloucester candlestick in the Victoria and Albert Museum as illustrated, *op. cit.* p. 166. J. Tavernor's *Dinanderie* gives a full account of the early Rhenish metal-artists. For ivory see author's *op. cit.* p. 168.

has in many cases a Romanesque carving, which is distinctly Norse in technique[1], as if in direct descent from the cross-sculpture. These tympana date from the first years of the twelfth century and are found almost exclusively in the midlands. Their animal carvings are of Norse idealism, which in its technique makes gradual passage into the dogmatic imagery of continental monasticism. The earlier imagery shows a fetish[2]—Christ appearing as a lamb, or a St Michael as a petticoated puppet spearing a knot-tailed dragon. Other doorheads give, not only the "Crucifixion" or the "Adoration of the Magi," the stock narrative pieces, but also the "Virgin and Child" and the "Coronation of the Virgin," subjects of doctrinal significance: even what is called "Christ in Majesty" is an exegetical declaration[3]. Thus the education of the sculptor was the admission of England into the current monastic culture, so that there came into the carving of English church fabric the subject-matter of continental art. And in the continuous progression of the mason's power for building purposes, his chisel gained expression for the themes of sculpture. He left the flat technique and developed more effective detail in the round, till by the middle of the twelfth century we reach figure-works definitely conceived as statuesque[4].

(*e*) Manuscript Motives

Still, up to the middle of the twelfth century, the faced stone, made smooth both internally and externally by a skin of plaster or gesso, was accepted: on its smooth silvery ground, wherever opportunity allowed—on the piers of doorways or the recessive

[1] C. E. Keyser, *Norman Tympana and Lintels*, gives many examples.

[2] See at Barton Segrave, Northants., S. Gardner, Pl. LXXI and Dinton, Bucks., Pl. LXX, "Souls feeding on the fruits of the Gospel"; also *Med. Fig.-Sculp. in Eng.* pp. 149, 155.

[3] See for illustration *op. cit.* pp. 171, 176, 195.

[4] *Op. cit.* pp. 198, 214.

orders of arches—every surface was set out by coloured patterns. Chevrons, billets, corbels, beak-heads, beads, pellets, that were the decorations of the manuscript page, were painted large on the body of the building. Since in many positions the effect of the colour would be enforced by cutting in the patterns on the stone, the building-mason acquired the habit of carving them[1]. Straight lines, zig-zags and billets were easy and of early execution; but by the middle of the century there came the elaborations of chequers and scrolls, carved eagles and "beak-heads" on the voussoirs of door arches[2], and finally the carved diapering of flat surfaces for the decoration of walls[3]. The capital of a pier, the plain breadth of which was Anglo-Norman economy, offered itself for a painting attracting the eye by its position and claiming attention. Like the initial capital of the manuscript it was a vantage-point for graphic design, seized on to establish the critical points of Benedictine dogmatism[4]. To enforce the story a cutting in of colour outlines, and then a modelling in salient relief, became expediency of craft. At Ely are capitals, some painted only, others with the devices carved and painted. At Romsey can be seen how in this way little figure-subjects grew common in the mid-twelfth-century elaboration of carving. In the translation of manuscript painting, the signs of the zodiac were worked up into all manner of symbolic fancies[5] and zoomorphic carvings which are the sign manual of the Romanesque sculptor. But also fonts were sculptured with subjects that were the statements of creed: at Barfreston the tympanum is a "Majesty" wreathed about with foliage in painter's style, but in the technique of an ivory carver[6].

[1] See S. Gardner, Pls. XXXVII, XXXIX, LXXIV.

[2] Pl. LXXIII.

[3] Pl. LXXII.

[4] See the capital from Westminster Abbey with the "Judgement of Solomon" in the author's *Med. Fig.-Sculp. in Eng.* p. 162 and other examples, pp. 93, 165.

[5] S. Gardner, Pls. LXXII, LXXV.

[6] Pl. LXXVI.

Together with the cloister paintings, bronzes and ivory carving passed into the hands of the Benedictine sculptors as models: the foundation of Gothic expression was laid in the monastery, so much so, that when religious thought in the twelfth century acted to suppress this grotesque luxury of animal carving (see on p. 46), the latest phase of Romanesque art was a revision and re-editing of the graphic arts of stone decoration[1].

The map facing p. xii gives the sites of the principal Anglo-Norman church-buildings and also of the first developments of Gothic masoncraft in England as discussed in the next chapter.

[1] See the author's *Med. Fig.-Sculp. in Eng.* Chs. II and III.

CHAPTER III

CLUNIAC AND CISTERCIAN, 1140—1215

E. LUXURY AND TEMPERANCE

(*a*) Succession of Monastic Ideals. (*b*) The Lordly Cluniac. (*c*) The Economic Cistercian. (*d*) The Canon Obligation. (*e*) Monastic Humanities. (*f*) St Bernard's Protest. (*g*) Cistercian Architecture. (*h*) The Evolution of Free Sculpture.

(*a*) Succession of Monastic Ideals

The vigour and competence of the Benedictine church-building claim for it the twelfth century. But art-competence becoming extravagant provokes reaction. An opposition arose and English work in the mid-career of its twelfth-century church-building discovers two issues at war with one another. There was an elaborate magnificence and, on the other hand, a temperate reserve, and these expressions may be entitled "Cluniac" for the *luxury*, and "Cistercian" for the *temperance.* Still under both designations they were forces of the Benedictine monastic civilization, and their antagonism and controversy belong to that generation, when in the Benedictine community the Cistercian ideality of religion was establishing itself against the Cluniac. The importance for English art lies in the combined outcome, for it established the national expression of English masoncraft. When the issue set up between the Cluniac and the Cistercian subsided, as it did towards the end of the twelfth century, church-building was found to be *English Gothic.*

In this bald statement the labels attached are not to be taken as exclusive, in the sense of crediting monastic orders, any more than bodies of *artifices* with particular creeds of arts. What is meant is that successive waves of Cluniac and Cistercian church-building gave the English artist his opportunity: on them he rose to his destiny. And this was so, although they had been French (or rather Burgundian) monasteries which at Cluny and Citeaux appeared on the European stage, in succession heading the movement of medieval religion. The sites of both are in that mid-European upland between the Seine, Loire and Rhone where is the watershed for Mediterranean and Northern waters[1]. But it was only as reconstructions or reformations of the monastic idea that they affected the actions of English artists. When twelfth-century monks set out an abbey-church, its design was one of practical use[2]. No renaissance of Art with a big A was in their mind—they claimed no prerogative or gospel of aesthetic culture. Indeed neither the craftsmen of Cluniac luxury, nor of Cistercian building-science, were as the Byzantine or Greek craftsmen of the early centuries had been—masters of a decorative style. So the Abbot of Cluny or the Abbot of Citeaux come into the story, not as artists or architects, but as the officers of the religious supremacy which the Benedictine theory of social improvement claimed for its order. Cluniac and Cistercian in succession dominated the material of English art, as the builders of English religion, not as apostles of culture.

(*b*) The Lordly Cluniac

The Cluniac was the earlier movement by a hundred years. Its distinction indeed dates back to the end of the tenth century, a generation or two before the Norman Conquest. Its mission, as the authoritative exponent of the Benedictine creed of life, had come to it at the end of the eleventh century, and grew out of the reputation of the first three abbots of Cluny who got a political backing. The Emperor, Otto the Great, in whose personality a Saxon kingship had been lifted to the dignity of

[1] Cluny and Citeaux are in the departments *Saône et Loire* and *Côte d'Or* respectively.

[2] S. Gardner, pp. 43 seq.

the secular headship of Christendom, became specially a patron of the Order, but also the religious head of the Church, the Pope, was its supporter. The Cluniacs obtained from Hildebrand many powers and privileges, and in the eleventh century Cluniac influence was spread widely in over three hundred daughter-houses, directly governed from the Burgundian abbey. They had Priories in England at Bermondsey, Lewes, Castle Acre, and Wenlock: Reading Abbey, too, was founded under Cluniac influence. Claiming the highest culture of the age, the status of the Order was advertised all over Europe in a magnificent housing. And as the mother abbey-church of Cluny was by the enlargements of the early twelfth century made the largest in Europe, with a quire extended into a complete basilican church beyond the main transept, so its plan of a double transept, adopted at Lewes in England, became a model for the premier English Benedictine cathedral at Canterbury[1]. So vouched for and illustrated, a Cluniac supremacy was established over English church-building. It was a luxury of magnificent Romanesque that architectural ambitions and culture established[2]. As the feudal lord had power over the revenue of his fief and expressed himself in the magnificence of a palace castle, so the Benedictine monastery assumed the prerogative of lordship and used the resources of its great estate in enterprises of abbey-building. A princely church architecture with extravagant ornamental luxury[3] became the established convention of church design, and to the end of its medieval style, despite reformations and vows of poverty, every community and order of the associated "religious" finally asserted fellowship with these first magnificent builders.

[1] The plan of Canterbury is given opposite p. 32.

[2] The widespread Cluniac influences can be illustrated from S. Sernin, Toulouse (T. G. Jackson, *Byz. Rom. Arch.* Vol. II. pp. 82, 83) and S. Iago di Compostella in Spain, G. E. Street, *Goth. Arch. in Spain*, Vol. I. p. 191. 1914.

[3] The English Benedictine versionings of Cluniac sculpture-luxury at Rochester, Malmesbury (S. Gardner, Pl. CXXXVIII) and Glastonbury are discussed in author's *Med. Fig.-Sculp. in Eng.* Chap. III.

(c) The Economic Cistercian

Yet, as we have said, there was another side of religious thought in the first half of the twelfth century, favouring a practical sense of building that aimed at being economic rather than luxurious. The Cistercian reconstitution of Benedictine monasticism arose in Citeaux with immediate daughter-houses at Clairvaux and Pontigny[1]. Their buildings became the insistent models for communities, who reproduced them in a wide circle of daughter-houses, so that Cistercian building was promulgated to Europe. It was, however, in England that its special importance for the Gothic development was acquired. An Englishman as it happened, Stephen Harding, had been the author of the Cistercian charter, the *Carta Caritatis*, or the bond of charity. By its statutes all the Cistercian daughter-houses obtained an equal temporal status, and the Cistercian abbots, coming together yearly in convocation under the presidency of the mother-house, regulated a uniform discipline. St Bernard of Clairvaux was the religious leader of his time and by his personality established Cistercian ideality in command of the thought of Europe. It was a moral supremacy as against the temporal assertion of the Cluniacs. To the creed of St Bernard were attached popular religious foundations from the middle of the twelfth century, and their special conditions created for their churches a practical type. For Europe generally was its expression of religious temperance enunciated, but it was specially for England that Cistercian *construction* developed in opposition to the elaboration of ornament. Building asceticism was conceived as the straightforward simple planning of square areas with an economic masonry of wall and window. Such continence of architectural style bred at any rate a vigorous manhood for English masoncraft.

[1] See F. Bond, *Goth. Arch. in Eng.* p. 599 for illustration of Pontigny.

(*d*) The Canon Obligation

Both Cluniacs and Cistercians being Benedictines, their successive control was the same course of monastic evolution that the Norman Conquest had initiated. The "reformed" manner of architecture was, however, in the latter half of the twelfth century not solely Cistercian. Various monastic, semi-monastic and semi-secular orders had sought the prestige of social usefulness, as a reaction from the lordly aloofness of the older Benedictines. The most conspicuous and popular throughout the twelfth century were those of the Canons—who were clergy of service to a church, instead of being vowed to a system of separate communistic life[1]. The Benedictine monk could be a layman, but a canon had to "take orders" as we say—that is, he was by profession a cleric, attached to special duty in connection with a special church. In England under the circumstances of the Conquest some cathedral churches were built for the services of canons at London, Chichester, Lincoln and Exeter. But though of secular use, yet in planning and masoncraft they followed the lines of the Benedictine erections so that at Chichester and Hereford we see to a great extent the monastic complexion that the original building assumed[2]. Indeed the obligations of the canon to his church had in the early centuries been interpreted with many differences. Towards the end of the eleventh century a discipline or "rule" of canonry called the *Augustinian* was promulgated. Thenceforward there were "Austin Canons," who, as associated under rule in communities, were called *Regular* canons, and were, in fact, monks as far as the architectural expression of their needs appears in building. Many variations of this rule had favour in the twelfth century: but that of Premontré, under its founder St Norbert, obtained distinction as of an ascetic strictness expressed in a

[1] See A. H. Thompson, *Eng. Mon.* pp. 159 seq.

[2] S. Gardner, Pl. CXI for Hereford.

church-building of the baldest constructional severity—as free from the gauds and luxuries of Benedictine masonry as any Cistercian fabric.

In England, towards the middle of the twelfth century, Premonstratensian influence was strong in northern building[1], so that its structural discipline of architecture is apparent. The canon orders however never obtained the resources nor reached the imperial distinction that the old Benedictine establishments acquired. In scale and circumstance the new abbey-building[2] could not vie with what even the less distinguished of the Anglo-Norman foundations had afforded. Of the Augustinian churches only one, that of the Canons of Carlisle, was cathedral in the twelfth century: most got their special importance in the late thirteenth and fourteenth. The churches of Bristol, and Christchurch at Oxford were made cathedrals by Henry VIII: but are of insignificant dimension compared with what at Ely, Winchester or Durham still witnesses to the resources of the first Benedictine institution[3].

But if the neo-monastic building was of smaller dimension, yet as an architectural movement its extent may be judged from the record we have of the Bishop of Laon, who we read built ten churches in twenty years—one for Benedict, four for Bernard (i.e. Cistercian), five for Norbert (i.e. Premonstratensian)[4]. Moreover there were active in building other institutions—such as those of the Gilbertines, an English order with canons and canonesses in one house. Also in England the military

[1] Alnwick, Blanchland, Coverham, Dryburgh, Eggleston in Northumberland or on its borders were Premonstratensian—the largest remains are at Easby or St Agatha's, near Richmond, which became an important house.

[2] Lanercost and Llanthony compared with Selby or Tewkesbury. See MAP OF SITES, Pl. II, also author's *Goth. Art in Eng.* pp. 85, 87.

[3] For illustrations of Augustinian building of the twelfth century see St Botolph's, Colchester, S. Gardner, Fig. 4; Christchurch Priory, Hants., T. G. Jackson, *Byz. Rom. Arch.* Vol. II. p. 234.

[4] See F. Bond, *Eng. Church Arch.* p. 17.

orders, Knight-Templar and Hospitaller, if not ascetic in constitution, had church Preceptories and were represented in architecture[1]. Thus by reason of their material conditions neo-monastic institutions were clients for what we may call, for short, a "Reformed" architecture in which the experimental building went on step by step under the stimulus of economical masoncraft away from the Benedictine Romanesque[2].

(*e*) Monastic Humanities

In the twelfth century all church-building was witness to the Christian humanities because life and thought were concerned in the struggle of religion to deliver civilization from the inhuman savageries that private warfare provoked. This was the acknowledged mission of the Church in Stephen's reign, and the foundation of monasteries proceeded as the protest of society: the peace of the Church was a power at hand to deliver men from anarchy. So if architecture in its castle-building expressed feudal despotism, in its church-building it expressed freedom, and this in the whole complex of religious institution. Equally in the ancient Saxon nuns' house at Romsey[3] and in the Gilbertine church of Malton, a free architecture materialized the hope of the age.

In its first stage, the expression of monastic authority had sought *beauty* as a temporal magnificence. So the Benedictine order claimed it in the abbey architecture of Durham, Ely and

[1] The Temple Church in London was built *c.* 1180.

[2] For the Hermits Mount Grace in Yorkshire, *c.* 1450, illustrates ascetic building at the end of the medieval story. The latter-day luxury of the foreign Chartreuses as of the Certosa at Pavia was never exemplified in England. The Friars—Franciscan and Dominican who also may be thought as eschewing building luxury in the consciousness of wider religious duties—came to us in the thirteenth century, but their building in England was on a small scale till after 1350, at which date (see p. 125 below) the conditions of medieval art were not favourable to the controlling influence of any religious order on architectural style.

[3] See for illustration F. Bond, *Eng. Church Arch.* p. 771 and plan p. 121.

Peterborough. But monastic reform thought it out as a seemly nobility of culture in terms of building. To mid-twelfth century neo-monastic philosophy preached beauty as the moral continence of the religious art. Yet one might picture the Gothic evolution as the last determination and the final award: for this was given as a "Judgement of Paris": the material queenship of art was the Hera of the Greek parable: the practical morality of it was the Athene: both yielded the prize to the intrinsic beauty of the masons' craftsmanship.

(*f*) St Bernard's Protest

So if to Cluny was ascribed the highest power of monastic pride in building, if to St Bernard's architecture came the sincerity of religious art, the achievements of Gothic were for neither. The Cluniac prerogative was magnificence: the church fabric claimed to be the foster-mother of painting, sculpture, and all the skills of metal work, glass and embroidery: and moreover to express as a lordly ritual the symbols of faith. There have been in architecture no such profuse and elaborate allegories of stone as were wrought on the twelfth-century church-fronts[1], and in England, as in France, mid-century doorways show riots of carving and fretted filigrees of sculpture[2]. Yet it was against these that St Bernard took up his parable in the well-known diatribe.

"What advantage is there in these ridiculous monsters—in that marvellous and deformed comeliness, that comely deformity! To what purpose are those unclean apes, those fierce lions, those monstrous centaurs, those half-men, those striped tigers, those fighting knights, those hunters winding their horns? Here a four-footed beast with serpent's tail. Here a fish with beast's

[1] Continental examples in author's *Med. Fig.-Sculp. in Eng.* p. 129, also T. G. Jackson, *Byz. Rom. Arch.* Vol. II. pp. 87, 88.

[2] English examples, S. Gardner, Pls. CXXXVIII, CXXXIX; also *Med. Fig.-Sculp. in Eng.* pp. 185 seq.

head. In churches we are more tempted to read in stone than in our service books—to spend the day wondering at such sights, than in meditating on the law of God[1]."

St Bernard in such words outlined a medieval morality for architecture—that it lay in the practical expression of the religious duty of service to God. The disciplines of *building*, not its gauds and luxuries, were the sanctions. And in so appreciating religious art, the Cistercian made labour the foremost contribution to aesthetic civilization. His lay-brethren—*conversi* as they were called—were *socii* of the Order; but not as secluded cloister-artists as had been the monk-craftsmen of the old Benedictines: they were herdsmen, cultivators—and moreover *builders*.

(*g*) Cistercian Architecture

The Cistercian colonies of labour civilized great stretches of country: we note their sympathy with natural beauty in the names of their foundations, Clairvaux, "bright valleys"—Strata florida, "flower banks"—Beaulieu speaks of a fair place—Fountains of bright streams. The Cistercian abbey sites are still those of a pastoral scenery with their meadows and hillsides reclaimed from desert roughness in the power of the labour creed of St Bernard.

The first obligation of these conquerors of the wild was to settle themselves, with presbytery and chapter as the centre of their monastic life; to cultivate their farm and build barns for harvesting its produce. After this proceeded the extension of their church, that under the discipline of economic usefulness became a practical building experiment. The Dissolution of monasteries left to ruin and decay the greater part of these reformed architectures[2]: still unroofed and battered they have an

[1] Quoted from G. G. Coulton's paraphrase, *Med. Garner*, p. 72. How St Bernard's homilies were to the point may be judged from the crypt carvings of *c.* 1140 at Canterbury. *Med. Fig.-Sculp. in Eng.* p. 164.

[2] S. Gardner, Pls. IV, XLII, XLIII.

eloquence of working efficiency, beyond what was built for the older Benedictines by masons conscripted into the service of the house, and continuing as a caste of decorative stone-cutters.

No doubt, at the outset of Cistercian building, this caste was drawn upon. But as the works progressed, the gauds of Benedictine masoncraft are seen dying out[1]. Elegance was born in the accomplishment of constructive skill: that is to say, Gothic architecture comes into being. Since a somewhat similar evolution was taking place abroad, the credit of it can be easily assigned to the Burgundian and Picard origins of the Reformed Orders. But these origins do not explain the English art—for if some Burgundian masoncrafts are found in the first Cistercian building[2] they disappear in the plenitude of the native craftsmanship. Technical craft is seen developed locally on the site of each Cistercian house so that the advances of structural expression were in fact attained in the body of the English craft. The planning of the reformed fabrics initiated a new era of scientific experiment in constructive economies, and the effects of wall arcade and moulding which we see developed at Fountains, Byland, Rivaulx grew to be essentially English[3].

(*b*) The Evolution of Free Sculpture

But when we pass from the Cistercian schooling of structure and reckon up the decorative schooling that masonry got in sculpture, then the continental connections grow evident: the pattern carving and zodiacal motives of the first Benedictine cloister crafts are seen giving place to the doctrinal figure-representation. The impetus to medieval sculpture had come in the

[1] Fountains, Furness and Kirkstall show, *c.* 1150, some stock Benedictine patternings, the best illustrations of which are in *Architectural Parallels*, E. Sharpe, 1848.

[2] See at Fountains, *c.* 1135, the Burgundian vault, S. Gardner, Pls. XLII, XLIII.

[3] S. Gardner, Pls. LXXXVII, LI; T. G. Jackson, *Goth. Arch.* Vol. I. p. 223. Roche Abbey in Yorkshire illustrates constructive economy.

crafts of metal-working and in the skills of painting, faculties exercised in the monastic cloister: the motives being such as could be conveyed in manuscripts, they were disseminated throughout Christian Europe. The setting and figure tracing of religious subjects (along with the patterning of diapers and the petty picturings of medallions) had their origin in the *scriptorium*[1]: their conventions were uniform throughout the whole area of European Romanesque. Yet graphic motives could be transferred to building only in as far as the chisel could compass them, and whether worked in the round, or cut in upon a line tracing, required skills beyond those of penmanship or the trivial chippings of an ivory. A mason's capacity for sculpture grows in a course of apprenticeship: in all parts of Europe it was the building achievement that exercised and stimulated the stone-mason's ambition. So figure-sculpture grew up as just an artificer's accomplishment in the twelfth century. Lost for eight centuries in Europe had been the making of a detached figure—the sculpture of a *statue*; it was come anew as an incident of church-building in all parts of West Europe—at first in flat relief and as the incised reinforcement of a painted subject, following the lines of the draughtsman's perspective[2]. But the mason as he grew in skill, instead of incising lines and making a pattern of his subject, began to round his forms and make sculpture of them. Bit by bit his modelling grew more forceful, until the action of the scene was raised above the ground, head and limbs were carved in projection, and finally the whole imagery stands free—the ground has disappeared: what was a scene has become a statue[3].

No doubt the suggestion for this evolution was the image of metal, ivory or wood now essential as religious furniture for the

[1] The writing-chamber attached to the Librarium in a monastic cloister.

[2] As the "Prior's" Door at Ely, see author's *Med. Fig.-Sculp. in Eng.* p. 206.

[3] See the English progress from flat to round, *Ibid.* pp. 186, 191, 198, 200. Also Rochester (S. Gardner, Pl. LXXVII), Malmesbury (Pl. CXXXVIII) and Lincoln (Pl. CXXXIX).

altar. But there is evidence that such images were, in the eleventh century, looked at askance as idolatrous. It may be fairly said that if the Greek statue and all its classic perfection grew out of a wood block—from the first a piece of detached expression—the medieval statue was not born of this parentage. It emerged from the matrix of a flat slab of building stone. And this not as any supreme artist's fancy or invention, but by gradual evolution in the practice of masons, in every place where an abbey-church was building. In Germany, in Italy, in Spain, in Burgundy, in Flanders, in South France and North France, and in England too, as the figures at York testify[1], the free statue was achieved during the latter years of the twelfth century. Though in the thirteenth century Gothic sculpture was to be a wonderful creation of the aesthetic imagination, it learnt itself as stone dressing. Its artistry came in the passage from the wall-concrete of the Romanesque *coementarius* to the dressing science of the Gothic *lapicida*—always experimenting in masonic economies, because stone was precious and each piece had to be shaped to its function in the building anatomy.

F. DISTRICTS OF GOTHIC EVOLUTION

(*a*) Northern Masoncraft. (*b*) Western Masoncraft. (*c*) The Conservative East. (*d*) Sussex, Kent and Canterbury. (*e*) English White-stone and Marble Craft.

The above sketch of the struggle of the mason with his material can be illustrated by defining four districts in each of which the English Romanesque gradually achieved its translation into Gothic. In each twelfth-century architecture obtained a different sense of masonic evolution[2].

(*a*) Northern Masoncraft

The whole north of England, defined by a line drawn from the Dee to the Wash with its northern border far into Scot-

[1] *Ibid.* p. 124.

[2] For the sites of principal building see Map, Pl. II.

land, was one broad area that after the Conquest was re-settled and brought into cultivation, very largely by the religious houses of the first half of the twelfth century. There had descended from Saxon Christianity only one great Benedictine monastery, that of Durham, with its connections. There were lesser Benedictine houses at Lindisfarne, Whitby, Finchale and Tynemouth, this last a cell of St Albans; but except in the Durham neighbourhood mid-twelfth-century building did not retain the Benedictine type; the general style of the masoncraft at York and Selby reflects the conditions of the reforming monasteries. From *c.* 1140 (when the Cistercian Fountains was founded) on to the building of Augustinians at Hexham and of secular canons at York and Ripon (*c.* 1180) we find a masoncraft of practical construction advanced in some forty or fifty buildings[1]. For this pure art of building the quarry is the key, and the robust character of northern work expresses its use of the big sandstones of the carboniferous grit. Cistercian building by ascetic rejection of the lavish surface-sculpture of Romanesque, elaborated a constructional art of arcadings and lancet windows, with a beautiful shaping of doorways[2].

(*b*) Western Masoncraft

As eager in its experiments and as productive of advance towards Gothic expression was the masoncraft of the Reformed monasteries in the western province of style that stretches from Chester to Bristol. Its chief area was a wide borderland along the Welsh mountains, "Marches" as they were called, in which new religious foundations obtained lands, and as English penetration proceeded built churches on both sides of Severn, Wye and Usk. In the service of monastic building, the oolites of Bristol were shipped into South Wales and across the Irish Sea to Dublin—

[1] See S. Gardner, Pls. XLII, XLIII, LXXXVII, also F. Bond, *Goth. Arch. in Eng.* pp. 102, 159 seq.; *Eng. Church Arch.* p. 747.

[2] At Byland and Rivaulx in Yorkshire, *op. cit.* pp. 13, 671.

but inland the sandstones of local quarries were in use especially for Cistercian building[1].

At Llanthony near Abergavenny is an abbey-building of 1170, which illustrates a distinctive Augustinian craft with less constructive energy than what the robust experiments of the northern counties developed. Its masoncraft had a lighter material, and specially elegant are the new ornaments of construction, that the western mason worked in the logic of his style[2]. Here more than elsewhere originated that speciality of the English Gothic, the enforcement of the lines of constructive intention, by soft successions of hollow and round. Of this district, too, was carved leafage in the spring of the capital distinguishing English work, as much as do its moulded arches, from the contemporary continental Gothic[3]. The pier development of western masoncraft had a significance for the development of English style and all these uses discover an advanced expression beside what was going on at the date, 1160—1180, on the east side of England[4].

(*c*) The Conservative East

They were central and eastern areas of England in which the original Anglo-Norman abbey-building had produced its monumental, though outside had been great monastic cathedrals, Durham in the north, Winchester and Canterbury in the south. Still the main body of Benedictine masoncraft had developed in the middle east of England where were set the

[1] Strata Florida, Dore, etc. See author's *Goth. Art in Eng.* pp. 156 seq.

[2] Ibid. *op. cit.* pp. 86, 87. For St Davids and Worcester nave see T. G. Jackson, *Goth. Arch.* Vol. I. pp. 180—183, and for Wells, p. 185.

[3] See Wells, Llandaff and Llanidloes in the author's *Goth. Art in Eng.* pp. 145—148, also F. Bond, *Goth. Arch. in Eng.* pp. 422, 423, 424.

[4] Christ Church, Oxford (Ibid. *Eng. Church Arch.* p. 779), Glastonbury (*op. cit.* p. 745). For piers, capitals, and moulded arches see author's *Goth. Art in Eng.* pp. 144, 145, also T. G. Jackson, *Goth. Arch.* Vol. I. pp. 186, 187, and F. Bond, *Goth. Arch. in Eng.* p. 424 and *Eng. Church Arch.* p. 469.

capital monasteries of St Albans, St Edmundsbury, Waltham, Peterborough, Ramsey, Colchester and Reading, as well as the monastic cathedral establishments of Norwich, Ely and Rochester[1]. The latter half of the twelfth century saw the completion of the naves of Peterborough and Ely, and there had continued in all the monastic establishments a very considerable building of infirmaries, and of enlarged refectories and offices[2]. So were fostered conservative masoncrafts: in such service, for a hundred years or more, bodies of masons and carpenters would be working under the charge of the Sacrist. Father and son, master and apprentice, rendered a continuing tradition of monastic expression so that the Romanesque solidities and zodiacal decorations were carried on almost to the end of the century in Mid-England[3]. Still though not in the front rank of advance the Benedictine masons had contributed to English style a developed habit of ranged arcades inside and outside their churches which while accentuating the continuity of wall surface reduced its substance.

(*d*) Sussex, Kent and Canterbury

The south-east of England made broadly a fourth district, in which, during the last quarter of the twelfth century, monastic masoncraft was transformed by advancing experiment into that specialized English building whose nature and expression of art will be the main subject of the next chapter. The significant monument remains to us in Canterbury quire, the rebuilding of

[1] Ely was cathedral in 1109. St Paul's, London, was a secular cathedral, on the monastic plan that matched the greater abbey-churches. See for Peterborough S. Gardner, Pl. LXXXVI; Norwich, Pls. XL, XLI.

[2] See the St Edmundsbury gateway, Pl. XXIII.

[3] A good deal of parish-church building at the hands of the monastic masons is conjectured for the middle of the twelfth century, as Castor, near Peterborough, S. Gardner, Pl. XXV; Stewkley, Pl. XXIV; Iffley, near Oxford, Pl. LXXIII. See for Northampton T. G. Jackson, *Byz. Rom. Arch.* Vol. II. p. 238.

which is recorded in all detail by a contemporary, so that, of all medieval work, its story is best known to us[1]. Kent and Sussex were most immediate to the continental church-building which in Picardy especially was advancing with great rapidity of masons' experiment towards the Gothic[2] developments that were taking place also in the Île de France, and in Champagne[3]. The Canterbury record informs us that a French master mason, William of Sens, undertook the rebuilding of the quire that had been burnt—promising to put it up as it had been built sixty years before. He did nothing of the kind: he could not, because in the first place, he was master of his own craft, as his works show. And secondly, he had as his assistants English masons, who already at Chichester and other places had got a science of building with new materials, especially the Purbeck marble of Dorset. The work at Canterbury is in touch with the big-stone science of vaulting, and at first piers and capitals are to the pattern of French masoncraft[4], but as it proceeds the handling is of another kind, and this predominates to make the architecture of Canterbury not French but the start of English Gothic[5].

(*e*) English White-stone and Marble Craft

The south-eastern craft was shaped and nurtured in economy by the general absence of local stone that could be got easily for the building of a great church. In the Middle Ages road conveyance of stone was difficult for its uses inland—whenever possible it was taken by water. It was economy for the monks of Canterbury to ship Caen-stone from Normandy, and Purbeck

[1] Good extracts from Willis' translation of Eadmer's account are given S. Gardner, pp. 43, 44.

[2] Illustrations are given of Senlis, Soissons and Noyon, T. G. Jackson, *Goth. Arch.* Vol. I. pp. 67, 73—75.

[3] For St Denis and Sens see *op. cit.* Vol. I. p. 38.

[4] See capitals, S. Gardner, Pl. CXVIII.

[5] Shafted piers Pl. XLV and marble base Pl. CXIII.

marble from Dorset, rather than to cart the Surrey sandstone across the weald of Kent from Godstone or Reigate. So the first practical work of the master mason, William of Sens, was machinery for the landing of seaborne stone at Richborough—his first constructions were the cranes for transferring it from ship to barge, so that it might be floated up the Stour to Canterbury. Now stone from Caen would, for ease of handling, be put on board in small blocks[1]. At Swanage too the *Marmor*, so called, was at hand to an anchorage and its pieces could be easily stowed[2]. Beds of from six to eight inches diameter were available, and the craft of turning and polishing them was native to the Isle of Purbeck[1]. Therefore, as an economy of building, shafts worked with bases and capitals ready for fixing were brought by sea. Thus by the nature of his material the English mason developed style, using a fine white-stone masonry in small pieces wherewith to build a great cathedral church, the pillar work of which was easiest got in making use of the special turning craft of Dorset marble. The two expediencies made an art of church-building in that corner of England which, if it was closest to the continent, was also the capital centre of English polity as in state so in church. The English Gothic mason entered into his domain of architecture[3] and to him surrendered the tied abbey-building crafts whose massive magnificence of style had envisaged monastic life and thought in the first century after the Conquest. The control of the new medieval craftsmanship was established in South-east England and spread from there[4].

[1] At Canterbury it is remarkably thin-bedded.

[2] The record of conveyance is *c.* 1170 for Durham Galilee, T. G. Jackson, *Byz. Rom. Arch.* Vol. II. p. 227.

[3] At Chichester, S. Gardner, Pl. CXIX. See for Temple Church, London, F. Bond, *Eng. Church Arch.* p. 17.

[4] For all the Gothic development see J. Bilson, *Beg. Goth. Arch.*

CHAPTER IV

THE ENGLISH GOTHIC, 1215—1250

G. EPISCOPAL BUILDING

(*a*) John's Reign and the Interdict. (*b*) Bishops' Building Before and After. (*c*) Salisbury and the Virgin-cult. (*d*) The New Architecture. (*e*) The New Sculpture. (*f*) The English Humanism. (*g*) The Wells "Judgement."

(*a*) JOHN'S REIGN AND THE INTERDICT

This chapter might be entitled "English and French masons in separation" because the creation of style, which is commonly called "Early English," was conterminous, but not homogeneous, with the Île de France creation of what may be called "Great Gothic." The political aspects of King John's reign account for the break away from the close continental connections that had subsisted in the monastic order of things. His kingship was no longer that of a continental power as his brother Richard's had been. Saint Louis as the successor of Philip Augustus had on the other hand assumed the leadership of European culture, and of this the French art was the expression. But while the French King's long reign meant a stability for the conditions under which the cathedrals of the Île de France and the immediate territories advanced to their consummate achievement the vexations and troubles of the English Crown made for twenty years a barren time for English building. Wars and civil tumults may often be prohibitive of art, but not always—for example the invasions and discords of Athens in the fifth century were instances to the contrary as were the thirteenth- and fourteenth-century faction-fights of Florence. War and Art are not necessarily antagonists, but rather allied energies—intervening tranquillity has more often proved the canker, and has heralded, if not induced, the decays.

In the case of the medieval art which in England was so essentially one of church-building, the ban of the Pope, called the *Interdict*, by which Rome claimed from 1207 to stop all masses and sacraments in England, necessarily closed down operations. Thus along with the flight of the bishops abroad there was in effect an interdict of the arts. When in 1217 the door was opened again to church-art on the return of the bishops it was with a changed outlook: for in the religious expression of life and thought it was now to be not the monk, but the bishop, who proposed and directed English building—so much the monuments of English architecture abundantly illustrate[1].

We have seen how the luxury and regality of Benedictine masoncraft had by the end of the twelfth century yielded to an art of reformed monasticism, which, in accepting the Cistercian and Augustinian economies of construction, made of them a science, and moreover a decorative expression which developed in wall painting, in glass and in foliage-sculpture. In this science were built or building *c.* 1200 the great quires of York, Wells, Canterbury and Lincoln. But it was all still of Benedictine, Cluniac or Cistercian tradition with expressions of monastic planning unchanged. The thirteenth century opens a new page of the art-record: the cathedral fabrics of Lincoln and Salisbury represent a new dispensation. As twelfth-century art had been monastic, so thirteenth-century was to be episcopal.

(*b*) Bishops' Building Before and After

A new style of building in the last years of the twelfth century had been associated with bishops. For example in Bishop Lucy's chapels at Winchester[2], Bishop Eustace's Galilee at Ely, Bishop Gilbert's presbytery at Rochester were additions

[1] Discussed in the author's *Gothic Art in England*, pp. 161 seq.

[2] See S. Gardner, Pl. XLVI.

made to conservative Benedictine monuments as if under some dictation from the diocesan authority. In the early years of the thirteenth century, at Chichester and Lincoln were enlargements of secular cathedrals carrying the English art of marble and white-stone far on in its career, with ambitions beyond those of monastic building, and moreover outside the continental features of Canterbury[1]. Near Durham Bishop Pudsey's chapel at Auckland is remarkable evidence (if it can rightly be assigned to him) that the old Benedictine schools of builders were replaced by new performers[2]. At York, the quire of Bishop Roger is left only in remains of the crypt: at Ripon is to be seen a small part of his building in the transept, but what is left of these late twelfth-century fabrics can be claimed as of a new régime of masoncraft[3].

It was in the last year of the twelfth century that the Bishop of Lincoln (St Hugh, as he was afterwards called) started his cathedral magnificence. His eastward planning was a somewhat fanciful variation of the monastic apse[4], and this before the end of the thirteenth century was superseded by the *Angel Choir* that we now see. But there remains the pier and vault structure of his quire and eastern transept clearly of English style and of the new order[5]. In 1218, and after, there followed successive buildings, the scheme of the cathedral being carried forward, enlarged and beautified under bishops who are historically famous as maintaining the English prerogative of national life. St Hugh, whose episcopal mastership dictated the fanciful apse-planning, had refused to countenance Cœur de

[1] Both seem built *c.* 1200; for Lincoln see T. G. Jackson, *Goth. Arch.* Vol. I. p. 199; for Chichester see S. Gardner, Pl. CXIX.

[2] The best illustration of the Early English Gothic of North England is to be found in Sharpe's *Parallels.*

[3] S. Gardner, Pl. LXXXVII for example of Bishop Roger's building.

[4] See T. G. Jackson, *Goth. Arch.* Vol. I. p. 201.

[5] See view, *op. cit.* p. 202.

Lion in his un-English levy. Next was Bishop Hugh of Wells, brother of the Jocelyn of Wells whose was the original conception of the great front there: an Englishman of West Somerset stock, he had stood by Archbishop Langton in the signing of the Magna Charta. And then succeeded the famous Bishop Grosseteste, the defender of the rights of the English church, a great scholar, and friend of Roger Bacon—by these bishops was Lincoln Cathedral designed and by their masons was it built as the expression of the new life and thought that the thirteenth century inaugurated[1].

(*c*) Salisbury and the Virgin-cult

No less does the planning of Salisbury Cathedral illustrate how the English episcopate had this mission in the first half of the thirteenth century, that English religious custom and English art were together of a distinction to be expressed and maintained in the building of churches. At Salisbury the two Bishops Poore were of a local English family—Herbert was the last with his cathedral at Old Sarum on the famous castle-hill: the next bishop, Richard, set his cathedral in its new site, the St Mary's meadow by the Avon, where it stands to-day. The seal of the chapter is still the "Madonna and Child": the shaping of the church dedicated to the Mother of Christ, is measure of how much the ritual cult of Our Lady meant for architectural distinction in English church-building. The Salisbury plan, put by the side of that of Amiens, shows architecture born in the needs of the time with no fancying of Gothic effects such as does the modern cathedral where Gothic pattern is avowedly regardless of twentieth-century facts. To the cult of the Mother of Christ England was specially dedicated, and accordingly the building out eastward of Lady-chapels was a prominent expression of popular devotion—for in these extensions the church diverged from the monastic types of the preceding

[1] See for plan S. Gardner, p. 46, and for details Fig. 23, Pls. XLVII, LXXXIX.

century. The innovation in the placing of Lady-chapels was not accepted in many of the Benedictine cathedrals. Thus Canterbury put the altar in the crypt; Rochester in the south aisle of the Nave. Durham in 1160 refused Our Lady near the shrine of St Cuthbert, but placed Her in the Galilee at the west end. Ely built its Lady-chapel in the fourteenth century as a detached building opening from the north aisle of the quire. Still many monastic churches had square-ended chapels built out, as those at Winchester *c.* 1200 superseding apses, or as at Worcester and Ely somewhat later. On the other hand in the secular cathedrals and more important canons' churches the thirteenth century made a peculiarly English feature of the long Lady-chapel, adding still further to the length of the English church—sometimes with a lower roof but often with a high-gabled distinction for it[1].

(*d*) The New Architecture

In the secular church-buildings of the thirteenth century were expressed the popular developments of the English ritual. At Salisbury the Wyatt works and those of his nineteenth-century followers have left to us the interior of the cathedral a somewhat lifeless travesty of its thirteenth-century art. The loss of medieval wall-painting and coloured glass is here made specially grievous to the eye by some worthless commercialisms put in their places. The Purbeck shafts are now black-leaded pipes set against white scraped stone—they dwarf and falsify the original ethic of the building art. In place of the now bare wall-faces, one saw full coloured painting on a black ground—while the silvery sheen of the glass in the windows gave it texture.

[1] See the author's *Goth. Art in Eng.* p. 228 for Chichester, also F. Bond, *Eng. Church Arch.* p. 749; for Hereford, *op. cit.* p. 87; for Salisbury, *op. cit.* p. 71. These were low-gabled extensions. Southwell (*Goth. Arch. in Eng.* p. 359) and Lincoln, S. Gardner, Pl. VIII, have the Lady-chapel extended to the full height, as do the chapel extensions of Ely, Worcester and Durham.

Still to be studied at Salisbury, however, is that English evolution of building-stone whose sculpture was as significant as the architecture itself. The carved pieces have lost the decorative accent that they had as colour-pieces, but one small portion of the original quire-screen (restored away by Wyatt) is to be seen in the N.E. Transept[1] and its tinted sculpture suggests a stage of art-instinct similar to that of the fifth century in Greece. The analogy may be carried further: as the acanthus was to the Greek artist, so to the English was the lily or iris flower, taken as the symbol of the Madonna—as if in the form of a living flower her divine gracious maidenhood could be enshrined in capitals and corbels. It has been a misnomer to call this "stiff leaf": it has the accent of joyous springing life which is the mark of the thirteenth-century figure-sculpture itself[2].

(*e*) The New Sculpture

The quick progression of thirteenth-century sculpture was prefaced by the wide distribution of the antecedent Benedictine luxury of ornament which had founded itself on the cloister crafts of metal and ivory. As explained in the last chapter architectural carving had its rise in the decorative scroll-works that the manuscript illuminator had fancied. The convoluted griffins and medallions of zodiacal beasts had been the meditations of a cloister culture wrapped in symbolic philosophy. But when Cistercian scrupulosity banished such raree show from the building scheme, the capitals of columns were fashioned as simple bells or just traced with springing leafage[3]. The abstention from complicated figure-capitals and arch-moulds of zodiacal pattern was a response of art to the neo-monastic

[1] See the author's *Med. Fig.-Sculp. in Eng.* pp. 230 seq. and 256 seq.

Ibid. pp. 260 seq.

Dore in the West (F. Bond, *Eng. Church Arch.* p. 546) and Byland in Yorkshire (*Ibid.* p. 506). French capitals develop (*c.* 1200) wreath sculpture: English not till *c.* 1240.

ideal: in the pride of its skill masoncraft elaborated foliages and the "dog-tooth" with crocket enrichment of mouldings[1] as structural accents. But even so it was a mason's training under the tutelage of a culture somewhat aloof and esoteric. To this day the Yorkshire abbey conveys the sense of a lodge in a wilderness; as if in its dedication to architectural forms of enrichment, and its discard of symbolical exuberance, it professed an art of refined negation—as a luxury of taste for the elect.

But the episcopal ideals were not so squeamish; they were for the populous centres of medieval life. The strength of the thirteenth-century building asserted the common right to a religious life, and the Lady-chapel was especially that of the people's religion. So in the motives of the cathedral mason there was an excursion into the high-ways and hedges of humanity compelling all to come in. Whereas Benedictine sculpture had been lordly and decorative, episcopal sculpture set itself to be a popular education, and consciously addressed the multitude rather than the philosopher. Leaving symbolism and cabalistic formulae, it took its Deity as it found Him in the hawthorn or iris, the spring of the daffodil stem and the unstudied beauties of form and colour[2]. Accordingly the points and vantages of building-stone were to be conspicuous now for the humanity of the sculptor's expression; his label-stops, and corbel carvings were heads of men and women: from this time forward the harping angels and the pleasant cheerful mysteries of the faith made his moralities[3].

[1] Good examples are at Byland, Jervaulx and Rivaulx, T. G. Jackson, *Goth. Arch.* Vol. I. p. 223.

[2] The development of capital foliage can be studied, S. Gardner, Figs. 26, 27, Pls. CXXIII seq.

[3] See the author's illustrations made from the photographs of Mr Arthur Gardner, *Med. Fig.-Sculp. in Eng.* pp. 253 seq. and 277 seq.

(*f*) The English Humanism

Significantly the thirteenth-century statue was to be worked to the likeness of real men and women, with the nobility and the beauty that religious thought pictured as the perfections of the man-subsisting God and the Divine but human Mother. The Madonna subjects, treated domestically, were the favourite themes of sculptors: "The Annunciation," "The Mother and Child," "The Divine Son crowning His Divine Mother" became obligatory for the art of church walls[1]: it was in quite a popular sense that doctrinal exegesis controls the sculpture of English church-building—as in the statued front[2] of Wells Cathedral for example. This broad arcaded façade[3] was built under Bishop Jocelyn, brother of the bishop, who was at Lincoln completing the transept there. The story of faith is set forth in ranges of statues and reliefs which show the English stone-sculptor as the sensitive interpreter of human expression[4]. The episcopal dictation of the scheme has ordered that the front shall be read doctrinally as the genealogy of Christ; on the south side the sacerdotal or spiritual lineage; on the north the monarchical or human pedigree: but the conception has the comfortable one of adopting the whole natural estate of mankind into the family of God. Bishops, Monks, Kings and Warriors, Ladies and Deacons make in effect a general population adopted as the whole body of the church[5].

(*g*) The Wells "Judgement"

The final crown of the composition is the "Judgement of Christ"—the resurrection of the "saints," for there is no exhibition of the "damned." The predominant motive of the whole front is the brotherhood of men, all sharing in the benefits of the

[1] *Ibid.* pp. 275, 281, 321. [2] *Ibid.* pp. 300 seq.

[3] S. Gardner, Pl. IV. [4] Pls. CXL, CXLI.

[5] The façade dominated the open green which was the cemetery of the city. See the author's *Goth. Art in Eng.* pp. 214, 215. The whole arrangement of the sculpture is discussed and analysed in *Archaeologia*, 1904, Vol. LIX.

Virgin-birth of the Saviour of mankind. One may trace the hands of many sculptors and a progressive course of execution: the sainted company of holy men and women are just a human English race—it is all something different from the doctrinally accomplished logic that, at Amiens and Chartres, ranges types and antitypes with scientific acumen.

The distinction suggests a specially English trend for theology in the first part of the thirteenth century, as may be illustrated by other examples[1] which have at any rate the distinction that they seem markedly rejective of the Cluniac theology. That had been specially prolific in what may be called the "diabolic obsession." Devils, monsters and the torments of the damned made interest in the "Last Judgement" as the working representation for the French doorheads—from Autun and Vezelay 1150 to Bourges 1250[2]. The "lost" state was no doubt doctrinally as logical for sculpture as the happy state of the "blest." But the English figures of Wells, Westminster and Lincoln manifest the joys only. There is almost a merriment in this thirteenth-century delivery of the sculptural mind: it was as in the fifteenth-century Renaissance of Italy. Moreover as in the early Attic statues there has come, too, for the English figure a gracious serenity of pose and a fine texture of drapery[3].

English sculpture too was in possession of an architectural sufficiency, as growing in the structure. If the statues of the French cathedral have the greater objective skill as idealizing human form for religious instruction[4], yet they are less satis-

[1] See the angel sculpture of Westminster in the author's *Med. Fig.-Sculp. in Eng.* frontispiece and pp. 262, 263, 321.

[2] For illustration of Vezelay see T. G. Jackson, *Byz. Rom. Arch.* Vol. II. p. 102.

[3] The statues on the Prior's Gateway at Peterborough are illustrated in the author's *Med. Fig.-Sculp. in Eng.* p. 337.

[4] Good photographs are in T. G. Jackson, *Goth. Arch.* Vol. I. pp. 114, 115, 124. But see the 50 plates, A. Gardner, *The Medici Portfolio*, I.

factorily knitted into the building surfaces, and while full of meaning dialectically, as mason's craftsmanship are open to criticism. The thirteenth-century statues at Chartres and Amiens are less part of the niches they stand in, and round the deep arch-moulds of the French doorways seem in a building sense incongruous. It is suggestive that statue drapery and arch-moulding in English work have their surface sections practically similar, making one texture of craftsmanship[1]. And it is to the point that so early in Henry III's reign the building-mason's capacity had become the dominant determining factor of art-advance, and that in this the Englishman was developing his own craftsmanship not that of the French mason.

H. THE MID-CENTURY BUILDING

(*a*) Early English Style. (*b*) The Squared East-end. (*c*) Window Gable and Vault. (*d*) Lincoln, Salisbury and Westminster.

(*a*) Early English Style

Politically the loss by the English monarchy of its French possessions, Normandy and Anjou, separated English from the French art just as the masons of the Île de France had established themselves as masters of the great building art of the French cathedrals. By the side, but not of it, was the craft of the south-east of England whose marble shafts, moulded arches and level many-ribbed ceilings matured in a fine somewhat over-dressed structure, with bossy sculpture. The fabrics of Lincoln and Salisbury[2] in the course of their sixty years building advanced the marble and white-stone style to the

[1] See S. Gardner, Pls. CXL, CXLI; G. G. Coulton, *Med. Garner*, p. 86, gives an illustration from the Chartres glass: it shows the sculptors working their statues in the building stone.

[2] See for Lincoln S. Gardner, Pls. VIII, LIV; for Salisbury, Pl. VI; also F. Bond, *Eng. Church Arch.* 71.

summit of its effect[1]. In the twenty years 1220 to 1240 it was current throughout England. As Gothic experiment, its outstanding distinction was economy of material, obtained in elaborate elegances of skilful mason's work. The dark Purbeck shaftings had a slender accent of column intention, set against the finished modelling of the Early English arch-moulding that was almost a drapery: with the spring of their sculptured capitals and the soft roundness of moulded abacus and base they have all a sort of feminine elegance—one might call it a womanly appeal against the robust muscularity of the French masoncraft. And indeed we read in the Metrical Life of St Hugh[2] that its author deemed the marble shafts of Lincoln to "stand round the great piers even as a bevy of maidens stand marshalled for a dance."

French Gothic is called logical for its expression of the structural mechanism, in the power of which the vaults were lifted to a height nearly twice that of English ambition. But the English mason had a building logic of his own in his thinning out of stone-masses, so that the English thirteenth-century cathedral with less material was generally half as large again in ground area as its sisters across the Channel. Tenuity of support followed on the need for openness and lightness inside and out. The English vaultings[3] comparatively low were abutted without the massive flying-buttresses, that on the French exterior make an impressive, but somewhat monstrous, scaffolding behind which the windows disappear as an external expression of the building purpose. But the wall of the English church, un-

[1] See S. Gardner for Ely quire, Pl. LII; Beverley, Pl. VII; York transept, Pl. XC; the quire of Fountains, Pl. LI; for the Nine Altars of Durham, T. G. Jackson, *Goth. Arch.* Vol. I. p. 242.

[2] Quoted from G. G. Coulton, *Social Life in Britain*, p. 472. Good examples of the English shafting are at Southwark, S. Gardner, Pl. XLIX, and at Chichester, Pl. CXIX.

[3] See S. Gardner, Fig. 56, Pl. XLVII.

encumbered by buttress excess, was opened wide for windowing, which with the grace of the Early English lancet developed effective compositions on the gable fronts[1]. In their broad wall-faces, arcaded and many windowed, English uses obtained an economic meaning for church interior and exterior alike[2].

(*b*) The Squared East-end

While architectural need as first administered by both Cluniac and Cistercian reformations had adopted the square-ended sanctuary for the convenience of simple building, yet abroad after the middle of the twelfth century the reversion to traditional apsidal terminations was nearly universal. In England, in the twelfth century, the monastic building of the west and north districts, where masoncraft was not immediately in the leading-strings of the Benedictine abbey tradition, had evolved for square-planned sanctuaries high-gabled fronts[3]. By 1200 the square east-end had become established as English custom for great churches of all kinds whether monastic or secular[4]. It was only under dictation from a controlling authority that after this apsidal chapels and *chevets* on the models of the continental church were built[5]. At Westminster Abbey this was on the whim of a royal aesthetic educated in France. In the planning of its quire by royal instruction Westminster Abbey was able to reflect the stupendous science of French cathedral-building—in which was worked out the logical expression of the chevet—in which by skeleton arches and a shoring of flying-buttresses the lighting of the sanctuary was achieved,

[1] See Pl. VII.

[2] For interior see Winchester Chapels, S. Gardner, Pl. XLVI; for exteriors, West Walton Tower, Pl. XXVI.

[3] Tynemouth and Llanthony both *c.* 1190.

[4] Rochester and Wells *c.* 1200.

[5] Cistercian *chevets* on the model of Pontigny, as at Beaulieu, for which a French master mason would seem to have been imported. See author's *Goth. Art Eng.* pp. 18, 169.

through the meshes of circling chapels. The Gothic building-logic is, however, just as distinctly enunciated in the broad window compositions that the square gables of English planning induced. Well-lighted areas for the eastward sanctuary were the paramount condition in the service of the sacred shrine, for it must be remembered that the altar in the faith of the medieval Christian contained the Deity. Not committed to the ambition of enormous height for the vault, the English mason had his light unblocked by the masses of buttressing that the support of the chevet-vault required. The wall breadths of a square end were immediate for stretches of arcaded openings, in which attenuated construction made for the economy of stone[1]. The substance of the wall, so reduced to a mere shell in the elegance of arched window-ranges, was still more honeycombed as spandrels and foiled heads were sculptured into a connected tracery—for example the resolution of the arch-head into a pierced stone-screen occurs with a definite accent of Gothic in the triforium at Salisbury, and then is repeated in the ranging windows of the transept[2].

(*c*) Window Gable and Vault

The detail of the development of Gothic window carving has been worked out in endless treatises, chiefly as ballast for the revivalist theories of modern Gothic. In medieval art tracery was the incident of an economic experiment. For, under the stimulus of tradition, the square-ended sanctuary seemed to English churchmen to give more space and convenience for chapels, and especially for the Lady-chapel: it was clear that the lighting and decoration of altars and retables could be well achieved by it, but also Saxon tradition and builders' economy were here coming together. The narrow lancet and the ranged arcadings of the English walls had grown into the expression

[1] Well shown in S. Gardner, Pls. LXXXVIII, LXXXIX, XC.

[2] Pls. VI, XCII, also Ely, Pl. LII, and Lincoln, Pl. LIV.

of the English triforium and clerestory[1] and then with the bringing of such arcadings under one arch came a carving of the heads into tracery. On the other hand the economics of French architecture were founded on the needs of its own national church-expression: abroad cathedral sites were in the cities, and could not command the spaces that the open sites of English building had vacant for extensions of chapels and Lady-chapel. The condensation of a city plan produced the *chevet*, and the *chevet* produced the flying-buttress and the height of the French vault—so were the two Gothics differentiated.

The French *chevet* with its encircling chapels determined height, not length, as its modulus of effect, so the window was needed as a simple combination of the *double* light with a head of simple quatrefoils[2]. The English quire and transept designed a gabled wall-face in which graded lancets were the natural expediency—the centre the highest. Thus was evolved the *three*-light and *five*-light window, and as economy of material progressed, the English evolution of tracery[3].

So was it with the English vault, its method developed in the lengths of the monastic nave, in the extended quire and projected transepts, long halls—all originally wood-roofed by English carpentry. So materialized the level ridge of English groining with its surfacing of continuous perspective, where extra ribs knit the whole ceiling together[4]. In the French vault this continuity receded behind the separate structure of the vault-bay, each a moiety of construction domed and complete in itself, so that we see the French interior as a succession of vaulted bays and not as a ceiled enclosure.

[1] For the progression see Pls. XCII, XCIV, XCVI, XCVII.

[2] See at Laon, Chartres and Reims, T. G. Jackson, *Goth. Arch.* Vol. I. pp. 87 seq. At Lincoln the "Angel Choir" of 1260 develops the *double*.

[3] See Hereford—triforium of N. transept, S. Gardner, Pl. XCVIII, and then Southwell Chapter-house, Pl. C: also aisles of Lincoln "Angel Choir," Pl. LIV.

[4] See for sexpartite vault, Canterbury, Pl. XLV, for quadripartite, Winchester, Pl. XLVI, for developed English, Lincoln, Pl. LVII.

(*d*) Lincoln, Salisbury and Westminster

The Englishness of English building can be well exampled from the great cathedral of Lincoln. This was no church of a monastic community, that needed cloister, refectory and dormitory and all the appurtenances of a great Benedictine house. At Lincoln the church by itself was, as in the French cities, the architectural unit. Yet they are the lengths and dispositions of an Anglo-Norman abbey-building that, rendered into English Gothic, in the process develop a series of square-ended gabled halls. Thus it is a cathedral composed of Saxon elements of church-planning and in touch with Keltic rather than with Latin Christianity. So too the English "West Front" at Wells, Salisbury and Lincoln has detached itself from continental expression[1]. The tiers of arcaded niches hold each its statue with the effect of an exterior *iconostasis* or station of imagery—a different artistic expression from that of the caverned cliff face of Amiens.

Salisbury Cathedral exemplifies most completely the English uses of building craft in external architecture. The west front unaccented with towers is subordinated to the pyramidal apicing of the composition in the central spire[2]. The gabled square-ended naves, the projecting transepts and the aligned chapels spread the base of the pyramid that stands free on its broad stretch of open meadow. Four times came apsidal planning into England. It came with St Augustine, but in a hundred years or so the Keltic square sanctuary crowded it out. It was authoritatively imposed on English builders in the Norman Abbey church-plan, but by the end of the twelfth century the secular, lancet-lighted, square-ended Lady-chapel replaced it: moreover when periapsidal endings were directly introduced on Cistercian models, they had no progeny in English soil. For the fourth time the fancy of a King, Henry III, an artist in culture and an admirer of the great French artist King, St Louis, brought the

[1] Wells, S. Gardner, Pl. V, Salisbury, Pl. VI. [2] S. Gardner, Fig. 7.

aisled and chapelled circle of the *chevet* to Westminster[1]. But with Westminster, as had been the case with Canterbury a hundred years earlier, English masoncraft triumphed over the continental dictation. For not plan, but craft of Purbeck-marble and moulded arch-section makes the art of the royal Abbey: it is no French church spite of its *chevet*, and there were to be no copies of its circling chapels in English building.

[1] See plan below.

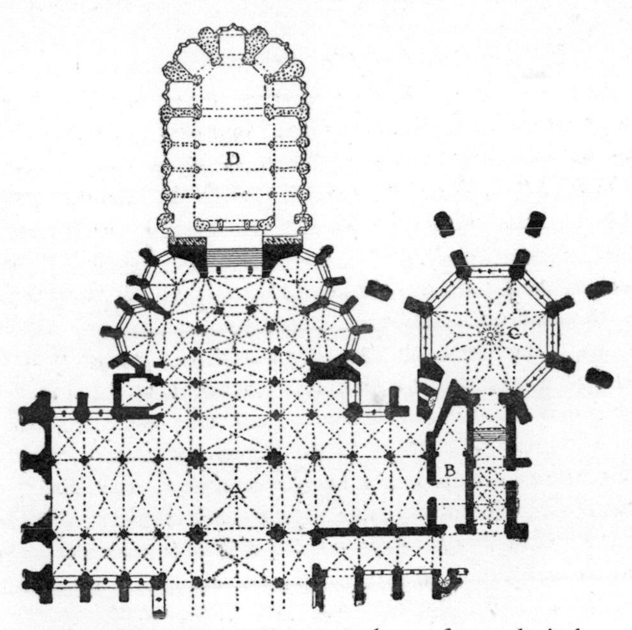

Plan of Westminster Chevet. Scale 100 feet to the inch.

A is Henry III's building *c.* 1250; see T. G. Jackson, *Goth. Arch.* Vol. I. pp. 262 seq. B is the "slype" called "Chapel of St Blaize." C is the Chapter-house. D is Henry VII Chapel *c.* 1500.

CHAPTER V

THE GOTHIC SUMMIT, 1250—1290

I. THE APPROACH OF ENGLISH AND FRENCH

(*a*) French Influence. (*b*) The Stylist Theory. (*c*) The Comacine and Freemason Theory. (*d*) The Building Competence in Expression. (*e*) The Joy of the Crafts. (*f*) Their Intellectual and Educational Capacity.

(*a*) French Influence

In the second half of the thirteenth century the French masoncrafts and the English came together: they have likenesses of detail and similar expressions which have impressed historians, who deduce the theory that at the summit level of the Gothic creation of style, since Paris was the creative centre, English masters were the immediate pupils of the Parisian. However, the limits of this approach have to be considered in view of medieval conditions. Since we moderns pay court to style, we gauge the distinction of a school or a period in our art values. We take shape, colour and proportion as the mint, anise and cummin of aesthetic law and since they were significantly French for church-building in the thirteenth century, their art, we say, must have been as a lawgiver's code for England.

But is not this putting the Île de France cathedral on a level with our "School-of-art examples"? as if its craftsmanship could be immediately and accurately copied by dutiful art-students. Certainly an easy way to view and review medieval art! If church-building was just the invention of artistic forms, one nation could learn its art from another. In the sixteenth century when the culture of the "Renaissance" did spread like a gospel, its evangelists might be pedants. But in the thirteenth English church-building had behind it a nationality and a *Gothic* of its own in no sense dependent on French propaganda.

(*b*) The Stylist Theory

The nineteenth-century ecclesiologists on the other hand, in the fervour of a *Revival*, claimed English Gothic as an indigenous recipe of religious art, the virtue of which was acquired by building English "lancets" and "traceries" and by carving "stiff-leaf" capitals, "dog-tooths" and corbelled shaftings[1]. This creed has on occasion found the French cathedral not *Early English* enough; too French some fervent ecclesiologists have feared! Still some of the rebound from *insularity* has been becoming pedantic. We have suffered this last thirty years from the travelled enthusiasms, which have found in the great French cathedral not only a wonderful building art but have made it an exclusive style. Adopting the learning and research of French archaeology, American philosophies of art have promulgated strict definitions, e.g. that Gothic is a system of vaulted structure, logically perfect in its usings by the French and such as could be the architectural test for Gothic execution elsewhere[2]. The theory proceeds that English church-building must have been as follows—William of Sens as a French architect brought Gothic to Canterbury: accordingly the style of the new quire became the model of design to English architects, who did their best to reproduce—but generally failed. Then when Henry III was building Westminster Abbey[3] some seventy years after, it was as a new "French" cathedral dictated to England—a reproduction of Reims, and English Gothic deferentially reformed itself on the new model. Such views turn on the conception of the medieval *architect*, as an individual, who, with the taste for design that a modern architect assumes, was able to beget a school of designers to practise in his style.

[1] So the Camden Society's publication *Handbook of English Ecclesiology*, Cambridge, 1847, p. 26.

[2] C. H. Moore, *Development and Character of Gothic Architecture*, p. 8.

[3] See back p. 71.

(*c*) The Comacine and Freemason Theory

A somewhat similar assumption is made by the esoteric clique of archaeologists, who explain the medieval building arts as those of a masonic society with a *mystery* that gave the monopoly of architecture. Some allege a secret signature as proof that all church-building was the output of a guild "Comacine" or "Freemason." It is to be found, they say, in such specialities of design as walls out of plumb, plans out of square, and other irregularities of execution such as a modern architect might introduce into his cut and dried designings in order to give picturesque unstudied curvatures to his lines of construction[1]. A hundred years ago, we were told that the Gothic cathedral was aisled in imitation of an avenue of trees, and was given ribbed vaults to suggest the branched perspective of a wood. Well—we know enough of medieval building to make us shy of so understanding the medieval artist. What we do find recorded in the documents or accounts of cathedral or abbey-church building is an easy open organization for ritual uses and practical purposes. Officials are appointed, and masons called together[2]. When names are mentioned, they indicate that the *dispositio* or general management was in the hands of the *cleric*,—in the monastery the sacrist, or for the king's works an official of state. Only occasionally has the record preserved the name of the working builder, *coementarius*—as for example *Robertus*, who was associated with Elias de Dereham as to Salisbury

[1] The interesting irregularities that have resulted in the planning and construction of medieval churches owing to piecemeal building, were discussed by the author in *The Architectural Review* of Feb. 1906, pp. 60—72.

[2] "Congregati sunt artifices," so Gervase of the Canterbury quire. See S. Gardner, pp. 43 seq.; *dispositio* is mentioned as to Elias de Dereham, *Lib. Rolls*, Hen. III, 1233, and as to Bishop Northwold of Ely, *Ibid.* 1252. See translations in Hudson Turner, *Domestic Architecture in England from the Conquest*, etc. Parker's edition, Vol. 1. Chap. v.

Cathedral, with the significant information that the said Robert "ruled the work[1]." In such a case the *mystery* or special function of *masonry* by which he exercised his appointment would seem to have been his capacity for a full-size setting out of the work. He ruled it for his *socii*—the working masons—as a foreman or clerk of work *rules* and sets out details to-day. The equilateral triangle, and the 3, 4, 5 square were his conjuring outfit—and it is interesting to see how the practical, but by no means mysterious, implements for laying out plain or arcade masonry have in many cases governed medieval proportions[2]. But modern practice of architecture asks for something more than this—it wants a conscious exercise of individuality. But since this is unrecorded of any person or of any class that medieval history mentions, an imagined secret society has to be improvised for it. For what our latter-day creeds of *aesthetic* insist is that art is distinguished by being outside common needs and practical accomplishments. Must we not reply that church-building was the common need, and its art one of universal accomplishment by the craftsmen of the Middle Ages? Its skills were therefore not what we *practise*, for architects and artists were not then such as we know them now.

In the official records of English medieval church-building there are connected with the great churches[3]—Elias de Dereham, as to Salisbury Cathedral in the thirteenth century; Alan of

[1] "Robertus coementarius rexit per xx annos." So Leland, quoted in Dodsworth's *Salisbury*.

[2] The doctrine of an esoteric modulus of proportion as governing design has lately been revived. It cannot be maintained for medieval work.

[3] The best analysis of the functions of the medieval "architects" is that of Wyatt Papworth in the *Transactions of the R.I.B.A.* of 1860—1861 and summarized in Gwilt's *Encyclopaedia of Architecture*, 1888. See however S. Gardner, pp. 43—46; also T. G. Jackson, *Goth. Arch.* Vol. I. pp. 264 seq. where are given names of recorded building agents from the eleventh to the seventeenth century, an insignificant list in view of the tens of thousands unmentioned in any record.

Walsingham, as to Ely in the fourteenth; William of Wykeham, at the end of the same century, as to Winchester; Reginald de Bray, as to St George's, Windsor, in the fifteenth century[1]. But, not as to any one of them does the record show them planners or designers of a building art. One can turn on this point with confidence to the authority of G. E. Street, himself of the strictest sect of religious architects, whose presentation of the case would adduce evidence, if it existed, to support his own preeminent practice. Reviewing the copious and distinct records of the Spanish cathedral-building of the Middle Ages, he sums up their information in the words, that though he thought it almost sacrilegious to doubt the existence of a separate class of architects—yet examination of the documents compels him to do so. "In fact the common belief in a race of clerical architects and in ubiquitous bodies of Freemasons seems to me altogether erroneous[2]."

(*d*) THE BUILDING COMPETENCE IN EXPRESSION

When builders build it is a constructive exercise: so when, or if, English masons adopted French forms (for example as to two-light windows, which were probably popularized for English work after Westminster Abbey), or if *vice versa* French masons took over certain English constructions (as for example at Amiens), it was for better building. Born in the open atmosphere of free experiment medieval art was robust in the natural health of practice. The joy of living "built the cathedrals, painted their windows, and filled their niches with statues." Their works were so of an obvious simplicity—a building was

[1] See author's *Cathedral Builders*, pp. 56, 57 (Elias de Dereham): pp. 74, 75 (Alan of Walsingham): pp. 85, 86 (William of Wykeham). See also as to Ely, G. G. Coulton, *Social Life in Britain*, p. 480.

[2] G. E. Street, *Goth. Arch. in Spain*, Chap. XXI. See also A. Jessopp, *Before the Great Pillage*, p. 23; as to Freemason, see G. G. Coulton, *op. cit.* p. 48.

fair because of its bright colour, for its stone was painted; for its smooth grace, for its stone was surfaced with a coating of gesso; for its sculpture claiming the privilege of natural sense of human shapeliness. The mason[1] worked not for dogmatism or intricacy but as the Greeks in the fifth century B.C., for joy. In the earlier sculpture of the English twelfth century the sacred mysteries had hidden themselves behind symbols as cabalistic signs: or more directly the pandemonic horrors of eternal fire had been used as an homily with hell-mouth tortures to decorate a tympanum or a capital. But now the thirteenth-century representation turned to the human joy of kindness, and the beauty of noble action. The charity, that had been scolded and repressed under the monastic régime, was wrought into stone. At the date of the carved angels of the Westminster transept[2] the thirteenth-century religion had given Europe the knight of chivalry in St Louis, and the devotee of humanity in St Francis. The knight's code of honour was humanizing warfare, as, too, the "Little Flowers of St Francis" were a delivery from dogmatism: so was it with the craftsman's art of cathedral-building.

(*e*) The Joy of the Crafts

It has been well said that medieval religion matured from the twelfth to the thirteenth century as a message of love. At any rate it seems so to voice itself in the building, sculpture and painting of 1200[3]. No doubt other voices—the ballad, the song and the tale of Romance—were asking to be heard, but the first to charm medieval society was the craftsman. As the immense church fabrics rose against the sky, year by year, at Lincoln or

[1] Author's *Med. Fig.-Sculp. in Eng.* frontispiece and pp. 85, 262, 263.

[2] No such sense can be sought in modern reproductions like the new transept-front of Westminster Abbey, or the nave and towers of Cologne Cathedral, which may be admired as scholars' exercise; but, as representing any art of the Middle Ages, they are merely diagrams.

[3] Mâle, *L'Art religieux du XIII siècle en France*, p. 454.

Salisbury, they figured in their stones a sacrament—a popular dedication to the service of Our Lady. The account of the wonderful building *c.* 1150 of the cathedral at Chartres has often been quoted[1]—how nobles, merchants, craftsmen, peasants gave—some money, some provisions—all gave labour, harnessing themselves to carts to drag the stone. Our Lady worked many miracles at her shrine at Chartres—but the great miracle was the human expression that the *work* of building wrought as its gift to the interests of life. For the century of great church-building the church-builder was educating his times in the sense that beauty has birth in workmanship—this may read to moderns as the dream-romance of a William Morris, but it seemed gospel to the times of St Francis and St Louis. In monastic building labour-questions had been argued with eternal damnation for the slackers: but in the thirteenth century there was to be partnership between man's work and God's service—"Whatsoever things are pure, lovely, of good report; if there be any virtue; if there be any praise"—so the free pleasure of his work was as much God's will as the craftsman's own. In Italy Franciscan ethics came as a spring birth: in France and in England the 1220 building of churches and their adornment were of the same philosophy. The everyday product of work found natural easy expressions—the arch-moulding was as the drapery of a queen; piers were sedate and elegant as maidens "marshalled for the dance" (see back p. 66); vaults were lifted as a sky-ceiling. But specially was man's image to be the joy of the thirteenth century—the right of the sculptor to make it so overruled dogmatic dictation. To be saintly was to be beautiful—as in Greek sculpture to be beautiful was to be divine: such was the first creation of a purely craftsman's art before by rule and prescription it was adulterated. Simple and innocent too was the colour practice of the thirteenth century, as we may see it in the manuscripts—its blues and reds on a silver ground,

[1] G. G. Coulton, *Medieval Garner*, pp. 100, 101.

as in the early works of church-glass[1] and of wall painting. But little of the latter has come down to us in a condition that can recover to our eyes the thirteenth-century colour-sense. At Chichester on the chapel wall of the Bishop's palace is a "Madonna and Child" attended by censing angels, austerely and delicately traced. (Frontispiece.) At Westminster is the more elaborate retable with figures of Christ and the Virgin and Saint, and medallions showing the miracles. Painted on wood panels upon a stamped gesso ground, enamelled in colour and gilt, this is a piece of rich and varied craftsmanship, such as a king could command[2].

(*f*) Their Intellectual and Educational Capacity

But while the crafts found their beauty in direct expressions there was a practical churchmanship on the intellectual side of religious interpretation. In the church's ritual, its masses, its obligations, its shrine-worship, its Sunday processions was church-plan evolved; so the types and antitypes, that were the doctrinal genealogy of the faith, made the sculptors' scheme. There has been a very thorough destruction of the English imagery, in which our churches once explained themselves, examples remain to us in no such numbers, as Chartres, Amiens and Reims have for the study of French art[3]. The most notable English works are the *Church* and *Synagogue* at Lincoln[4], both headless, but magnificent in their drapery; also the *Abbot*

[1] See S. B. Saint's drawings, reproduced in H. Arnold's *Stained Glass*, p. 44. At Chartres the thirteenth-century glaziers took their harmonies directly from the surrounding flower meadows. Restorations and revivals miss this simplicity and make either mud or fever of coloured glass. Such is the verdict when we see the "restored" examples at Canterbury (where half the work is modern) or at Lincoln where the author saw the old sapphire blue thrown on the ground and trampled to fragments by the "restorer."

[2] See W. R. Lethaby, *Westminster Abbey*, pp. 262 seq.

[3] See A. Gardner, *French Sculpture* (Medici Portfolio); also W. R. Lethaby, *Medieval Art*.

[4] Illustrated in author's *Med. Fig.-Sculp. in Eng.* p. 325.

and *Prior* upon the gate at Peterborough[1] are statues of distinction; and the reliefs of "Angels" in Lincoln quire and in the Westminster[2] transept are specially English.

These English arts, where they survive, exhibit an educational competence on its three sides—literary or doctrinal exegesis—scientific or material embodiment of practice—and thirdly artistic or creative suggestion as exalted by form and colour. The art display of a cathedral had for its generation a meaning unrecognized by picture galleries, or our shows of arts and crafts. The printed page has now for four centuries instructed us—we never lose its directive suggestion in schools, in libraries, in the thousand newspapers and magazines, that are our educators. But this was non-existent in the thirteenth century: the medieval craftsman gave knowledge to all the world in his cathedral-building—as master of craft he was *magister artium* too. While sculptors, painters, glaziers, metalworkers, goldsmiths, imagers, marblers, entailers, carpenters, masons and engineers appear in the records as all just *artifices*, yet their works were the compass of their time and ruled its life and thought.

There is evidence that in France the building masters of the mid-thirteenth century had social status, in this representative position as well as by their immediate reputation among their fellows. The memorial slabs of master masons of Reims and Amiens represent them as of rank by reason of their *craft*[3]. But they were not as we reckon them now architect-artists. Some 200 years afterwards in Italy the *artist* was discovered, as a social lion, the companion of princes. In the thirteenth century it would be by reason of his cathedral-building that the French master mason[4] was esteemed a commodity of repute,

[1] *Ibid.* p. 337. [2] *Ibid.* pp. 4, 262, 263, 271, 273.

[3] See W. R. Lethaby, *Med. Art*, Chap. x.

[4] One, Villars d'Honcourt, went to Austria; his sketch book has survived and been published in facsimile. It shows an absorption in figure-work

of immediate export to Spain, to Hungary, to Cyprus and to Sweden. And so was promulgated a new architecture superseding the continental Romanesque in which had moved Benedictine monasticism.

J. THE PARTING OF THE STYLES

(*a*) Italian and English. (*b*) Westminster Abbey and the King's Connoisseurship. (*c*) English Building Craft and the Chapter-houses. (*d*) At Lincoln, Old St Paul's and Exeter.

(*a*) Italian and English

The wholesale replacement of national art by French was not operative in two most marked nationalities of the thirteenth century—the Italian and the English. It may be suggested that Englishman and Italian had detached themselves from European culture each in his own art-evolution. Whereas Central Europe, with its shifting and mixed partitions of Charlemagne's Empire, remained an amalgam soft to the imprint of the stabilized civilization that the French kings created in the Île de France, the Italian communities in their peninsula had the Latin tradition of an art haloed with the imperial *aura*. In the fourteenth century the Italian craftsman adopted, by right of birth, classic style, claiming an individual responsibility for the artist that was to be the knell of the communal crafts of the Middle Ages. The English mason had likewise a birthright in his insular tradition with a right to be eclectic. The commanding achievement of his Anglo-Norman building had its issue in Early English Gothic, and this although, in 1250, the close connections of London and Paris in the intercourse of feudal ties made for reciprocity[1]. There certainly was a free

and building mechanics, rather than in what we call architecture. See G. G. Coulton, *Social Life*, etc. p. 477.

[1] Henry III, brought up in the Court of St Louis, held Aquitaine, as a vassal of France.

passage of workshop usages, and we must recognize similar determinations of building problems. Thus Henry III's building of Westminster Abbey was one in which the approach of English to French style was close; while at its date at Rouen and Amiens, as well as at Coutances and Dol *c.* 1250 there appeared very English masonries[1]. But another half century found the two no longer together, so separate indeed, that if continental art apart from Italy was as it were Frenchified, yet English Decorated made a distinct fashion, one that was to grow by way of Brittany and Flanders into that last French style—the Flamboyant.

(*b*) Westminster Abbey and the King's Connoisseurship

The building of Westminster quire has given us the consummate example of English style, for we find in it the crisis of our Gothic. In the first place was its significant assumption to be national not as a monastic, but as a regal enterprise. Secondly in this new field a new sense of craftsmanship comes into being, overshadowing the ancient religious dedications of art-service. Kings' craftsmen were not builders but shop-men, and in such appointments the status and opportunities of the English artist were altered.

The accounts of the Westminster work, for the year 1253 when the quire was finishing and the transept was being built, are preserved in the Rolls Office[2], and we may read them as the passing away of the impersonal artist. For this quire-building at Westminster was no longer the ordinary achievement of a monastic or episcopal career: but here was the King the client of architecture, and for him the king's master-workmen

[1] As that of Johannes Anglicus *c.* 1267 at St Urbain, Troyes, E. Lefèvre-Pontalis, *Champagne Méridionale*, p. 37.

[2] The large roll is in full, G. G. Scott, *Gleanings from Westminster Abbey*, pp. 231 seq., but the smaller fabric-roll is given only in part, p. 252. An entry, not quoted by Scott, speaks of statues *ad tascham* probably Chapter-house Annunciation figures. See the author's *Med. Fig.-Sculp. in Eng.* p. 320.

executed its dainties. We have state documents naming special artists: there was brought from Rome *Peter the Roman* to execute the Cosmati mosaics on the shrine of Edward the Confessor[1]. In the Edward I accounts of executors appointed to carry out the memorials of Queen Eleanor, for each of the Crosses the artists are named[2], sometimes in the old fashion just as *coementarius* (builder), but in one or two cases as *imaginator* (a figure-artist) or goldsmith (worker in bronze). There has come into existence the individual artist, in the execution of craft luxuries, as king's craftsman.

This itself is indication—that architectural initiation had passed from the ecclesiastic as a Churchman, though it might pertain to him as a Lord. Though it was for a monks' quire, not abbot but king was client. Westminster quire was built as might be the Mosque of a Mogul or the Tomb of a Fatimid Sultan. Edward the Confessor's shrine was asserting an ancestral rather than a religious piety—the motive of a royal mausoleum[3].

Henry III seems all his life an ardent memorialist, figuring in stone most of the members of his family. At Westminster the effigies of the English kings were begun with his own figure in bronze; but at his ordering would seem before this the Purbeck marble of his father "King John" at Worcester, the freestone figure of his uncle "Richard Cœur de Lion" at Rouen, and that of his aunt "Queen Berengaria" at Le Mans. The Liberate Rolls 1254 mention the King's directions to Dorset and Wilts., that a marble figure of his sister, the Queen of Scotland, be put on her tomb at Tarrant in Dorset. His connoisseurship in the arts appears abundantly at Westminster,

[1] There were two *Romans*, father and son. W. R. Lethaby, *Westminster Abbey and King's Craftsmen*.

[2] Hudson Turner, *Roxburghe Tracts* and *Archaeologia*, XXIX. See author's *Med. Fig.-Sculp. in Eng.* pp. 342 seq.

[3] A. P. Stanley, *Memorials of Westminster Abbey*, Chap. III. See author's *Cath. Build.* p. 63, for Boyce's fine drawing of the shrine.

as for example in the Roman mosaics—significantly too as to the plan of the abbey-church itself with its adaptation of French cathedral-science[1]. His interest in all operations of building and details of decoration may be read (*Liberate Rolls*) in the injunctions that accompany his orders for works to be done at his manor houses[2].

(*c*) English Building Craft and the Chapter-houses

Yet while the fabric of the abbey-church, following the planning, has French bay-mechanism and French flying-buttresses, still as a work of art it is English masoncraft wrought by the Purbeck marblers and with the English habit of white-stone cutters[3]. The distinction is profound—by 1250 the French had matured the ethics of the vault skeleton—in its morality obliterating the wall for the service of the constructional thrusts of vault support. The English mason on the other hand conceived his Gothic in the wall, and in the refinement of arch-structure as part of it. Dissolving substance into piers and arches, his experiment went on to a lightness of slender shaftings, of delicately moulded arch-lines, and to the foliated piercings of arch-heads in the ranges of the triforium and clerestory. So in his efforts the English mason worked, not to heights of vault but to breadth of open expression[4]. It was at this crisis or moment of summit, that each in the quest of masonic refinement French and English approach one another —when Westminster Abbey was building[5]; when at Salisbury,

[1] T. G. Jackson, *Goth. Arch.* Vol. I. pp. 270 seq.

[2] Such as "I will have it done though it cost a hundred pound." See Hudson Turner, *op. cit.* (Parker's edition), Vol. I. Chap. V.

[3] In the Westminster accounts of 1253 the *marmorarii* and the *cissores alborum lapidum* are separately entered. See author's *Cath. Build.* pp. 61—66; also T. G. Jackson, *Goth. Arch.* Vol. I. pp. 262, 274.

[4] For illustration of English style see S. Gardner, Pls. XCVII, LII, LIV.

[5] F. Bond, *Goth. Arch. in Eng.* p. 379.

the cloister and chapter-house were in execution; when Bishop Bridport's tomb there was sculptured[1]. For at this date too in France chapels were added at Amiens, Soissons and Noyon, that might, except for their French setting, have come from English church-builders.

Henry III's building at Westminster has its significance in being attached to Westminster Hall; for in the Abbey-Chapter the English Parliament met, and from it state papers were dated as in the Palace of Westminster. Specially English in plan were these chapter-houses, polygonal halls vaulted to a central pillar at Lincoln, Westminster, Salisbury and Wells: in them mason-craft attained its highest English economy. At Westminster one sees it in reflection of the English national constitution with the three estates of the realm represented in the circumstances of the building.

English art ceasing to be monastic or episcopal obtains the sense of a political mission: Seculars for their cathedral-building took over the palace architecture of chapter-house and cloister[2], and in doing so claimed a state dignity. In his governmental offices each representative Bishop at Salisbury, Wells or York seems expressing a new policy of art—its view to the world was to be the princely aristocratic one for church and state alike.

(*d*) At Lincoln, Old St Paul's and Exeter

At Lincoln, where had been the earliest of the secular chapter-houses[3], was also a quire enlargement of the latter part of the thirteenth century. It was for the shrining of St Hugh behind the high altar—as the Confessor had been shrined at Westminster—that there were schemed the five bays eastward that have got their name from the "Angel Choir." The

[1] See author's *Med. Fig.-Sculp. in Eng.* p. 77.

[2] For Salisbury cloister and Lincoln chapter-house see author's *Cath. Build.* Pls. 8 and 9.

[3] For chapter-house interior see F. Bond, *Eng. Church Arch.* p. 335.

angels, sculptured in relief above the arcades, are on the same scale and pattern as those at Westminster and like them are remarkable for their expression of English art. On its masonic side the immediate diversion of English style away from the French is marked. Immediately succeeding in date to the Westminster work, Lincoln architecture has a contrasted breadth of archway and window, a full rather than lofty system of piers, a broad modelling of mouldings and a rich wreathing of leaf-sculpture. Along with the uses of marble that had been distinctive of earlier style has come an enforcement of English textures, a superabundant sense of the qualities which had made our first Gothic distinct from the continental[1].

In the case of the London Cathedral there seems a leaner use of masoncraft, to judge from Hollar's prints, which were made in Charles I's time before the Fire of London. But though the great quire of St Paul's was built shortly after that of Westminster, it must rank as assertion of English style against French[2]. Characteristic is it, too, as London work at the end of the thirteenth century—for in it we may read, how city conditions worked when medieval building had no local quarry to draw from, so its manners of stone-usage were of introduced craft. In London masonry was necessarily one of shop-artists for whose craft were imported stones of decorative distinction from many places[3]. Yet in St Paul's quire these city-bred stylists were under no servitude to the French modellings of Westminster; the square east end[4] of the metropolitan Cathedral takes nothing from the *chevet* of the royal connoisseur;

[1] S. Gardner, Pls. LIV, CLIV; for angel sculpture Pl. CXLII.

[2] Author's *Cath. Build.* Pls. 14, 15.

[3] From Caen in Normandy; Purbeck in Dorset; Reigate in Surrey; Dunstable in Bucks.; Huddlestone in Yorks. As to the sculpture in these stones see author's *Med. Fig.-Sculp. in Eng.* Book III.

[4] See plans and elevations as taken from Hollar's prints, F. Bond, *Eng. Church Arch.* pp. 3, 4, 5, also p. 674.

yet with other great Cathedrals that of St Paul's makes secular assertion of episcopal dignity in regal chapter-house and cloister.

A third enterprise that at this date occupied English masoncraft was the rebuilding of Exeter Cathedral the great church of the west of England. Its quire was begun before 1279 and still remains a remarkable example of English architecture[1], despite the defacements that "restoration" has perpetrated during the last fifty years. The original workmanship here was of a quality unsurpassed, and though the finely wrought texture of west-country masonry, as was still in evidence fifty years ago, is much obliterated, the broader aspects of the fourteenth-century accomplishment may be recognized. Significantly English is the expression of the level, many-ribbed vault, whose low broad spans are abutted by only the single-arched flying-buttress. Also the resolution of wall surface into lace-works of tracery, together with the rich compositions of leafage and sculpture are distinct of the English genius, and were perfected with a wonderful delicacy of chisel-craft[2]. That this was church-furnishing rather than church-building was symptomatic. The mason's sense of style lay in his workmanship—his power over his chisel to give the texture of a romantic religious expression such as lay in the heart of the lordly Bishops of Exeter. The masons of Rouen were on the church of St Ouen, working out under French conditions their own evolution of style[3]. But very differently conceived was the English west-country technique of building, broad and full, with no sense of what at Le Mans or Beauvais had been the stupendous creation of a

[1] Sands's engraving of Exeter quire, valuable as made from a drawing by S. Rayner before "restoration," is in the author's *Cath. Build.* Pl. 17. For its dates see A. H. Thompson, *Exeter Fabric Rolls*, to be published shortly.

[2] See S. Gardner, Pls. X, XI, LVI, CI, CXLIV, CXLVII. Across the Channel Exeter masoncraft is to be seen at Tréguier, in Brittany.

[3] For St Ouen in comparison with Exeter see T. G. Jackson, *Goth. Arch.* Vol. I. p. 176.

fibrous fabric of stone engineering. English chiselling, nurtured in "Early English," was to pass into elaborations of the "Decorated" motive, as a church-furnishing trade[1]. But so it marks the close of French influence on European architecture. A new gospel was being preached in Decorated crafts, and as English style went on from Salisbury to Lincoln, to Exeter and then to Bristol, all that King Henry's quire had Frenchified at Westminster was as an interlude—the whim of royalty.

[1] See Bishop Grandisson's Ivory Triptych opp. p. 112. The expression of Decorated craft as an aristocratic religious culture is there illustrated. As Bishop of Exeter 1327—1369 Grandisson was "grave, wise and politick" and ambassador "at the courts of all the mightiest princes of Christendom."

CHAPTER VI

FIRST YEARS OF ROMANTIC ART, 1280—1310

K. ENGLISH DECORATED

(*a*) The French Building after 1280. (*b*) The English Dominance of Style. (*c*) Church-furnishing and its Craft of Aristocratic Display. (*d*) The Decorated Examples.

(*a*) THE FRENCH BUILDING AFTER 1280

The last twenty years of the thirteenth century and the first ten of the fourteenth made an era of high accomplishment throughout Europe in all the arts of church-building. English style had enriched itself in give and take with French master masoncrafts, and on the continent generally the French cathedral was setting a pattern to Gothic builders. Yet in the France of this achievement there had come a curious architectural paralysis of effort. The activities, in which the great cathedral had advanced to the summit of its Gothic art, died away. The years 1240 to 1280 had been those of the political ascendancy of France but the balance shifts with Edward I's reign—the English rivalry had been declared and by 1300 English masoncraft began to take the lead in Europe.

The intestinal warfare in the French territories cannot have affected the prestige of their arts for, at any rate, the half century of which we are speaking. Indeed from 1280 to 1330 French style was accepted throughout Europe: the Paris workshops were, till the Flemish superseded them, the centre of an art-furniture trade, religious and secular. To be "of Paris" was the gauge of accomplishment and an hall-mark in the commerce of ivories, paintings and enamels. The French sculptor in his figure-work had a *naïveté* and piquant naturalism that can be judged from the Madonna on the south porch at Amiens[1]. But for all that

[1] See the Medici Portfolios *French Sculpture of the Thirteenth Century*, by A. Gardner, Pl. XXII B, also author's *Cath. Build.* pp. 67, 68.

the building enterprise of the Île de France becomes scant —indeed *La Sainte Chapelle* of the King's Palace was almost the final achievement of the Parisian masters of the thirteenth century. At any rate there was an indolence of building beside the English activity, and it was not till some two hundred years later that in the great cathedral area French invention flares up in its brilliant after-glow of Flamboyant—in the light of which churches left as half finished in 1300 obtained their spires and west fronts[1].

(*b*) The English Dominance of Style

On the other hand this first half of the fourteenth century, if ineffective for French art, was a notable period of the English. In the two generations that followed the accession of Edward I, in 1272, there came enlargements and completions, that have constituted the bulk of the external architecture of our cathedrals. Our twelfth-century monastic churches have often doubled their area by their eastward extensions of the fourteenth. Towers and spires at Lincoln, Salisbury, Ely, Peterborough, Lichfield and Wells, were the conspicuous architectures of the "Decorated" century[2], remaining to this day in evidence of English style. In all this the French master mason, though he was currency in most parts of Europe, did not run in England. But neither, on the other hand, did the Italian Gothic that Giotto[3] and the Pisans practised make contribution to English art: it was a good two hundred years after 1300, that Italy graduated as Art-schoolmaster to Europe.

The connections that were immediate for English art lay in the industrial cities of Flanders, which had now become the emporium of Europe. It was near the close of the fourteenth

[1] See T. G. Jackson, *Goth. Arch.* Pls. CXXIV, CXXVIII, CXXXII for the *c.* 1500 spires and west towers of Rouen and Chartres.

[2] S. Gardner, Pls. XXVII, XXVIII, XXIX.

[3] See illustrations, T. G. Jackson, *Goth. Arch.* Vol. II. pp. 209, 224.

century that the lordship of Burgundy absorbed Bruges and Ghent, and in political expansion made a wide market for Low Country products. In the early years of the century however the Flemish arts of church-furnishing would seem not invading, but rather going to school in England: and so to English art belongs the half century between the French building art and the Flemish trade-art, because in the aristocratic affluence of English church-building there was brought into being our Decorated style, whose phase has no corresponding place in continental examples.

(*c*) Church-furnishing and its Craft of Aristocratic Display

This English art was a stone-furnishing one on the big scale of church-masoncraft. As already described, the quire of St Paul's in London was the work of shop masonry—a development of city image-work in the materials of building[1]. At Exeter and York too the provincial basis of Decorated style was its caste of city-workers, whose crafts had flourished in cathedral-furnishing, for the service of an ecclesiastic aristocracy. For now the chapels and chantries of nobles occupied the aisles and blocked the floors of cathedrals so that churches became practically mausoleums—caskets or shrines of the family pride, that had religious sanction by right of birth.

The secular nature of this memorial art, despite its religious profession, can be gathered from the heraldic ornaments—shields and badges of knighthood, that qualify it in the first years of the fourteenth century. At first such worldly devices are used as personal identifications merely[2]. But in the latter two centuries

[1] One indication of this appears in the detail of the latest (13th century) Purbeck-marble effigy-work, see author's *Med. Fig.-Sculp. in Eng.* p. 585.

[2] The Eleanor monuments, *c.* 1290, have the heraldry of her lineage. See S. Gardner, Pl. CLVI. The Cantilupe Shrine at Hereford has knights and shields, Pl. CLX. The Percy monument, *c.* 1320, at Beverley, Pl. CXXXI, though of a lady has similar sculpture.

of Gothic building the heraldry obtains so much the place of honour that in English churches sculpture and painting seem almost to disappear as religious offices. The Christian symbols and the sacred texts get repeated as formalities, but workshop faith had passed to pedigree as its creed. The circumstances of the fourteenth century engineered this curious relaxation of the religious bond of art. Following the lead of the King at Westminster, great families appropriated projects of church-building. The Augustinian houses were specially annexed[1], so much so that their religious establishments were all of a piece with the baronial. It was indeed a church militant in the fourteenth century—one of warrior bishops, and abbots who had knights in fee. Monasteries were maintained as fashionable retreats, and their guest-houses were counted as the clubs, where met a gay society of knights and ladies.

In the requirements of such patrons craftsmen flourished. *Decorated* was a style of practised variety and romantic invention, of splendid colour and lavish sculpture, left to us now in the walls of our churches or as witnessed by the fragments of retables and quire-screens that are in our cathedral museums[2]. Its more durable record has survived in the tombs and monuments of the aristocratic ecclesiastics, the bishops and abbots whose chantries block the arcades of many of our cathedrals. At the Dissolution the chief function of many great churches was thought to be their preservation of monumental erections, and as compared with continental examples we are fortunate in the preservation of these highly ornamented chapels that were the English speciality[3].

[1] The Bruce quire at Guisborough and the Berkeley quire at Bristol for example.

[2] T. G. Jackson, *Goth. Arch.* Vol. II. pp. 64, 70, 71; also S. Gardner, Pls. LVI, LXXXI, CXXXV, CXLVI.

[3] *Ibid.* Pls. CLVIII, LVIII, CLIX.

(*d*) The Decorated Examples

What English art achieved and what it signified from 1280 to the Black Death of 1348–9, can be read in traceries, crocketed canopies, and pinnacles. The record has been much damaged: for the Augustinian abbey-churches are now mostly in ruins. Still the architectural background of Decorated style has evidence in churches of secular foundation—whose collegiate quires were rebuilt late in the thirteenth century, the naves being carried to completion in the first half of the fourteenth. Thus Exeter Cathedral, as already described[1], was built in luxurious fashion by a series of aristocratic bishops, notable Princes of the Church, and in its fabric was wrought the finest workmanship that English craftsmen ever achieved. This of late years has been much maltreated, while at Lichfield, another monument of Decorated art, the original workmanship has suffered even more completely[2]. York nave with its chapter-house is characteristic architecture of the period, though there is little now original: the quire was a later work, outside the limits of the Decorated era[3]. Some Benedictine abbey-churches that joined in the fashionable magnificence of quire rebuilding illustrate its period, such as the Milton Abbey in Dorset, or as following the fall of the Tower at Ely, the quire and Lady-chapel there. Selby abbey-church in Yorkshire had a splendid preservation of what the Yorkshire guilds of stone-carvers could accomplish[4]; but the fire that burnt the roof of its quire has lately been made the occasion of some poor parodies of the original art. At Ely the Lady-chapel has as yet escaped complete restoration[5]. In a general way these buildings illustrate a shift of style from constructive competence to the furnishing dexterities which in their

[1] See back p. 87; also for illustrations S. Gardner, Pls. X, XI, LVI, CI.
[2] F. Bond, *Goth. Arch. in Eng.* p. 369.
[3] Author's *Cath. Build.* Pl. 11; also S. Gardner, Pls. LVII, CVI.
[4] S. Gardner, Pl. XII. [5] *Ibid.* Pl. CXXXV.

action as craft monopolies make the second chapter of the fourteenth-century style. But its first competence had been the romantic expression of aristocratic chivalry, as will be now discussed.

L. THE EXPRESSION OF CHIVALRY

(*a*) The Eleanor Crosses. (*b*) The Growing Individuality of Art. (*c*) Effigy Sculpture from Statant to Recumbent. (*d*) Castle and Palace-hall. (*e*) Secular Art in Quire and Chapter-house. (*f*) The Decay of Building Expression.

(*a*) The Eleanor Crosses

As has been said, it was a royal patronage of the arts that acted at Westminster and played its part, too, in the new quires of Lincoln and Exeter. But, when, as at Westminster, the knight's tomb succeeded to the saint's shrine as motive of abbey-church furnishing, royal authority had a new rôle. As Henry III had been an artist, Edward I, on the other hand, was a fighter. Knighthood was the princely art to him, and so in his reign craftsmanship took service in the ranks of chivalry. In the state accounts we read of his devotion to his Lady, expressed in the very remarkable set of monuments, which on the death of his Queen, Eleanor of Castile, were set up wherever in the funeral procession from Lincolnshire to Westminster her body had rested for the night[1]. Though in the form of, and with the name of, "Crosses" they are secular expressions, and interpret the revolution taking place in thirteenth-century life and thought. In their art the religious types and antitypes of doctrinal exegesis were no longer engaging the sculptor; but his theme had become the faith of chivalry, the Knight's homage to his Lady.

[1] Author's *Med. Fig.-Sculp. in Eng.* p. 643, also pp. 74, 99. At Geddington is now the most original monument. See S. Gardner, Pls. CLVI, CLVII, CLXIII.

So, too, the Eleanor tomb, in Westminster quire, figures the shields of her royal descent and lays her beautiful effigy under a saint's canopy[1]. It meant, at any rate, a growing interest in monumental display when for the making of the Eleanor crosses were enlisted the most famous sculptors of sacred images, and the figures of the Queen were fashioned as the Madonna. It was a turning point like that by which Greek sculpture passed from the religious content of the Pheidian circle, to the personal ideality of a Praxiteles or a Scopas—the goddess took shape as a woman.

(*b*) The Growing Individuality of Art

The conditions of the craftsman shifted when he was engaged for his skill in tomb-making. Gothic expression began to dethrone the religious forces that had lifted it to the supreme place it held in medieval civilization. For when, and as, church-building was losing its practical faculty, the Mayor of the palace of art was usurping the King's function. Hitherto individual artistry had been unrecorded—because in church-building, as Matthew Paris wrote, the glory was that of the Abbot, not of the executant. So the names of artists were of no consequence—art-faculty was not recognized, and the mason of the thirteenth century wrought his building-stone and his statue indiscriminately: both were his work as *coementarius*, and his carved figure was only a stone to be set.

Now, however, the accounts of the Eleanor trustees[2] mention the payees for the cross-makings by name, and by distinctions as craftsmen. One of them Alexander of Abingdon has claim to be what we call an Artist with a personal style of figure-work: he is entitled *imaginator*, that is a statue-maker, working figures in stone, bronze and wood. Still it was the craftsman

[1] E. Blore, *Monumental Remains*, No. 1.

[2] Given in full by Hudson Turner, *Roxburghe Club Publications*. See discussion of them in author's *Med. Fig.-Sculp. in Eng.* pp. 341 seq.

rather than shopman; his craft that of a goldsmith, maker of church ornaments and of the images of the altars. So at Florence at the same date, the trecento goldsmith was painter, metal-worker and sculptor in one. The faculties required for art grew into recognition as capacity for figure-work, and then could establish themselves apart from their constructive associations. Contemporary with the Eleanor crosses were those famous Westminster tombs which in their monumental distinction of high-gabled canopies are like nothing else in Europe. The riding knights in the trefoils of the gables are witness to the replacement of the religious conscience by the chivalric: the effigyist has indeed carved angels at the warrior's head, his servitors to carry his soul to Paradise[1].

(c) Effigy Sculpture from Statant to Recumbent

However, secular interests in monumental figure-work had for some time found place in churches. Abbots and Bishops were figured on their tombs no doubt as official saints: then we see in the first half of the thirteenth century Knights of the religious orders given military effigies. In both the evolution of artistic expression is significant at the end of the century. At first the dead prelate or abbot had been figured in his saintly quality—niched and upright, as Apostle had been drawn in manuscript or carved on ivory tablet. In the line of this spiritual genealogy the bishop was sculptured on his slab as if standing—with his benediction hand in the gesture of blessing, the other grasping his pastoral staff. But as the mason grew confident in his sculpture sense of imitative realism, the standing pretence became indistinct in his mind: to his art the memorial figure on the slab was recumbent lying in state with a cushion under its head and the drapery falling on the slab[2]. When kings and queens, and then lords and ladies too, were so sculptured, they were as asleep, awaiting resurrection in their mortuary chapels.

[1] S. Gardner, Pl. CLVIII.

[2] See author's *Med. Fig.-Sculp. in Eng.* pp. 584 seq.

The craftsman's art rose to its occasion; it is a living knight that sleeps on the slab at Salisbury. The Knight-Templar, as in the Temple church, is also lying on his back, but alive with martial alertness; he is sculptured cross-legged as if quick to spring to his feet, when the trump sounds for Armageddon. His shield is on his arm, his hand on his sword; at Westminster, equally watchful, Crouchback and Valence turn towards the altar with folded hands[1].

So with the ladies—at first they are figured as Madonna images, flat as in a drawing. But soon they become Sleeping Beauties, in the garb of aristocratic society—with the effects of drapery carefully studied, and in the attitudes of courtly bearing[2]. As with the figures of the Eleanor crosses, the expression of effigies was in noble posture—what had grown to grace in the artists' service of the Madonna was now translated into a secular distinction.

In another twenty years the tombs of the great can be seen encroaching on the sanctuaries and altars at Westminster, and just so the achievements of heraldry crowded out those of religion in the workshop arts of the second quarter of the fourteenth century[3]. For already in 1290 chivalric devotion was supplanting religious when for the monuments of Edward I's Queen and of his companions in arms the craftsman found the occasions of his art in the external pageantry of lordship, in colour and gaiety, in the romance and energy of knightly display[4]. Thus the apogee of the medieval tomb came as the

[1] *Ibid.* pp. 588 seq. For sleeping knight, p. 607; for martial, pp. 592 and 611; for Westminster, p. 652, also S. Gardner, Pl. CLVIII.

[2] Aveline at Westminster, Pl. CLVIII, also author's *Med. Fig.-Sculp. in Eng.* pp. 598 and 642 seq.

[3] Badges and coats of arms became after 1350 the commonplaces of sculptural motive, see p. 138 below.

[4] Froissart's Chronicles give the atmosphere of this art of 1300. It had its reverse; but so have the ideals of other times, as witness the League of Nations and coincidently the Russian and Irish horrors.

entry of art-commerce into the religious precinct and by this same passage medieval religion itself was ushered into a new era.

(*d*) Castle and Palace-hall

In Edward I's military campaigns the nobles of his court won their spurs, and in the fourteenth-century military architecture, as in its monumental, the romantic evolution of the building crafts expressed the new functions of the craftsman[1]. The Edwardian castles in Wales as at Caerphilly, Conway or Carnarvon reached as practical an expression of the military craftsmanship, as the knight's effigy of 1300 had done of the sculptured reality. The concentric castle with its triple wards, its inner and outer gate-house materialized the military experience of Edward I's Welsh wars. But if this fortress-type—as the culmination of medieval science—met the requirements of military life and thought before the invention of gunpowder[2], it was also the artistic expression of its time in what we call Romance. Those rings of machicolated towers that stand against the sky are as a pageant castle that Merlin might have conjured. In this as in all developments the expression of architecture was in the fourteenth century that of a social culture fed on knight errantry.

The church-building crafts were busy too on halls and guest-houses for the lodging and entertainment of knights and ladies. Households moved from manor to manor over the country, and it was as customary to be put up in a monastic house as to-day

[1] Castle- and church-building were on one plane of capacity. It was for his expertness in the former that William of Wykeham got his appointments, in the credit of which he grew to be the notable building ecclesiastic of the latter part of the fourteenth century, see pp. 76, 120.

[2] See A. Harvey, *Castles and Walled Towns of England*, pp. 17, 18, also Chap. VII. A picturesque description of a feudal castle of the fourteenth century is quoted in Hallam's *Middle Ages*, 1868, Vol. I. pp. 320, 321, from Monteil, *Histoire des Français des divers États*.

it is in an hotel[1]. We find bishops with half a dozen palaces, and establishments in each. The dimensions of the episcopal hall with its state apartments show the extent of a bishop's company. Under the medieval conditions of trade the sustenance of a great house was supplied only from the immediate local sources; when the provender of one manor was exhausted, Lord or Bishop moved on to another with retinue and household. Especially the King and his Court travelled continually about England, and had quarters and entertainment commandeered for the royal company. So the head of a religious house had to play the part of host to a distinguished circle of guests, and his *métier* was that of a courtier. Apart from the Christian virtue of hospitality, Bishops and Abbots were themselves great officers of state, with a regiment of knights and squires at command. On occasion Bishop and Abbot were found heading armies in the field, and as frequently as any other noble they went hunting and hawking. The manners of building would shift ecclesiastic to palatial function in reflection of such a society, and indeed on bishops' palaces now were spent the revenues of sees[2]. The Bishop of Lichfield, Walter de Langton, *c.* 1300 built the most magnificent house in England of his time. It was as assumption of lordship too that gatehouses and encircling walls ennobled monastic establishments[3].

[1] Peterborough Abbey built a "Knights' Hall." At Boxgrove Priory in Sussex a Guest-Hall, built for Edward I, has lately been allowed to fall into ruin with its fine sculpture a cock-shy for boys.

[2] The Bishop of Lincoln had some three or four palaces built or enlarged in the last years of the thirteenth century. At St Davids are the ruins of what was built by Bishop Gower *c.* 1330, T. G. Jackson, *Goth. Arch.* Vol. II. p. 70. At Wells the Bishops' Halls attached to the Palace are those of a great establishment on the scale of the Warwick or Ludlow building of Castle Halls.

[3] Notable monastic gateways were built for St Augustine's, Canterbury, and St Edmundsbury, *c.* 1300. At Easby and Kirkham in Yorkshire, and the Ethelbert Gate at Norwich are other examples of this century.

It was the dignity of "crenellation," so called—the right of fortification granted by the King—but moreover it was provision for garrison quarters of men-at-arms.

(*e*) Secular Art in Quire and Chapter-house

In such buildings fourteenth-century style has gone into the *world*—it was no longer dedicated to any sense of monastic withdrawal. The Augustinian churches were an evidently aristocratic display of church-building. Characteristic quires were added to most of the churches, Regular and Secular, large or small, that were served by Canons: many Benedictine houses followed with similar extensions. Most of these Decorated quires are however now in ruin[1]—that of Carlisle, the Augustinian church that was made cathedral on the old foundation, has remained in service: for the Regular churches were very generally dismantled at the Dissolution. At Ripon and Howden the Seculars have had better fortune, in them we get note of the rich handling of the fourteenth-century masons—of broad windows in which stone is interlaced—of tower-like buttresses gabled and pinnacled, with internally a florid fancy of canopied arcades and sculptured doorheads[2].

In exhibition of ecclesiastic luxury were the chapter-houses and cloisters of Canons already mentioned—in them were promoted constructional experiments for the English mason. The earlier chapter-halls, *c.* 1300, following those of Lincoln and Westminster were vaulted to central pillars. But at Thornton, Southwell and York[3] was obtained an unobstructed area—the

[1] Guisborough, Kirkham, Bridlington and Howden in Yorkshire. The best illustrations are in E. Sharpe's *Parallels* printed in 1840. F. Bond, *Goth. Arch. in Eng.* has reproduced many of them.

[2] For illustration see author's *Goth. Art in Eng.* Chap. VIII. Selby (exterior and interior) is given, S. Gardner, Pls. XII, CXXXIII. Exeter (exterior and interior) Pls. CI, LVI—the work in these cases being *c.* 1300—1335.

[3] St Paul's, London, had its chapter-house with open area.

pier being dispensed with—and here was a solution of the vault problem that had an important issue for English work. Also the cloisters of the Decorated period contributed, with their many-ribbed and well-bossed ceilings—all in the service of luxury. In such glazed and enclosed corridors at Norwich or St Albans monastic life accepted the worldly issues of domesticity, comfort and display. An architectural prettiness rather than a sculptural dignity attaches to the Decorated boss-sculpture of the cloister ceilings[1]. Life-size treatment is replaced by anecdotal decoration. As architectural mason-work the boss and crocket carvings of the fourteenth century are specially English by their wealth of figure-work; yet the high purpose of economic singleness that animated each individual figure-piece of the earlier art is lost. The art of sculpture was become *genre* in the building: it was also to do so in the image —for supplied as shop-figuring image-work forgot its original architectural content. The mason remained to the building as a carver of fancy arcade-works, in which structural sense was subordinated to the pretty traceries of line and foliage: his thirteenth-century right to make architectural imagery the voice of his art was taken from him[2].

(*f*) The Decay of Building Expression

As we have said the rebuildings of the cathedral quire of London[3] and of the nave of York[4] are representative works. The expression in either case was that of expert city craftsmen, engaged to minister to a lordly caste, whose pursuit of the decorative romance of pageantry was its master-motive. In this

[1] For illustration of fourteenth-century boss and corbel sculpture see author's *Med. Fig.-Sculp. in Eng.* pp. 380—389.

[2] A comparison may be made between Lincoln, S. Gardner, Pl. CXLII, and Ely, Pl. CXXXV. Selby capitals are shown Pl. CXXXIII.

[3] F. Bond, *Eng. Church Arch.* pp. 4, 5, 674.

[4] S. Gardner, Pl. LVII. See also F. Bond, *Goth. Arch. in Eng.* p. 82.

sense we must take the loss of feeling for structure that is significant in the London quire, in the York nave, as in the York chapter-house too and in the Lincoln cloisters, all works of the first quarter of the fourteenth century. It can be noted that their ceilings, though still of the form of stone-vaulting, are not masonry, but ribbings and boardings of oak in direct imitation of the stone structure[1]. Such is a pageant device—the make up of the scenery of a building romance, like the paste-board pavilions and castles of a tourney-show, or as the caskets modelled like churches that were made to carry relics in processions. In fact now begin to be elaborated those minute renderings of a church front or porch, that resulted in the canopied gable, crocketed and pinnacled, to be then used, tier above tier, as a commonplace of every decoration[2]. The most significant of such insincerities was the miniature spirelet or tabernacle, a medley of traceries and canopied niches, that after 1300 appear in all the crafts of the Gothic decorator, stone, wood and metal alike, regardless of the ethics of materials. The interests of constructional competence surrender to those of decorative variety. Lines of fluent curvature replace those of arch tracery—the architectural spacings become those of fancy, multiplied, fretted and frilled, cusped and crocketed—till with pinnacles and little decorative gables there are set up doll's-house miniatures of construction. So in the life-history of art do passions run to seed in architectural dotage, as Chapter VIII will illustrate.

[1] First at Lichfield, and also advised by Henry III to expedite matters at St George's, Windsor. See the St Albans ceiling of quire, author's *Med. Art in Eng.* p. 357, for Selby, p. 358.

[2] S. Gardner, Eleanor Cross, Pl. CLVI; Lincoln Tower, Pl. XXVIII; York Nave, Pl. LVII; the later fourteenth-century uses are shown Pls. LVIII, LXXXI, CLIX.

CHAPTER VII

THE SECOND ERA OF ENGLISH ROMANTIC ART, 1310—1350

M. CRAFT LUXURY

(*a*) The Ecclesiastic—Lord and Statesman. (*b*) Aristocratic Personality in Costume. (*c*) Fashion in the Fourteenth-century Effigy. (*d*) Decorated Motives of Romance.

(*a*) The Ecclesiastic—Lord and Statesman

The first decade of the fourteenth century was accentuating certain tendencies of art as of English civilization. The revolution of society, that, as events worked out, matured in the great pestilence of 1348—1350, was to re-arrange the relations of art to life: and this, although the mutation of thought that lay behind the changes of religion, came to be effective only after a couple of centuries. Roughly and widely stated, as regards architecture, it was art's compass-swing from church-building to house-building. The year 1307 was that of the death of Edward I, and the reigns of his two successors brought into action interests antagonistic to feudalism and monasticism. The struggle of society was to escape from the medieval formulae, though church-building in its emphasis of craft-skill was still to be the prominent expression of social well-being. For the fourteenth century was still giving high social dignity to the ecclesiastic; Abbots and Priors were prelates and bishops, and as such the acknowledged officers of the realm. John Stratford, Archbishop of Canterbury, was Lord Treasurer to Edward II and Lord Chancellor to Edward III. And as warrior as well as statesman, the Archbishop of York led an army against the Scots, in 1310, as did the Bishop of Durham a few years after. The highest positions in state administration were held by such ecclesiastics from 1325 to 1350. In this period bishops of Hereford, of Chichester, of Lichfield, of Lincoln, of Rochester, of Worcester, were state officers at one time or another. The most magnificent princes of their time were John Grandisson, Bishop of Exeter; Walter Langton, Bishop of Lichfield; and William Edington, Bishop of Winchester, the last being Lord Treasurer and Lord Chancellor of England at the time of the Black Death. All were great builders; but inasmuch that in their service Abbey-churches and Cathedrals were become expressions of state-dignity, architecture was passing from its religious dedication—its *métier* was to be official and social in response to new ideas; though this was not fully realized for another century.

(*b*) Aristocratic Personality in Costume

Meanwhile Sculpture was aristocratic and ecclesiastic, for the art impulses, which the fourteenth century developed, ran together as one movement. A convenient illustration of the artist's absorption in personal issues is afforded by his record of dress fashions. In the twelfth and thirteenth centuries costumes had been carved and painted with a practical simplicity, that was as innocent of design as was the gift of artistic handling. The tunic had been the accepted garment alike for men and women in the same social grade, so much so that in thirteenth-century representation the sexes can hardly be recognized as habited distinctively. For example, the figures of kings and ladies at Wells are carved with close-fitting tunics, with loose long girdles and with similar cloaks[1]. Youths and maidens in the thirteenth century wore their hair long, and only when figured with head covered, does the "lady" in her veil differ from capped "noble" or crowned king. Still there was this concession to sex, that with medieval modesty the lady never shows her ankles, and rarely the tips of her shoes. On the other hand office or ceremonial was distinctively habited, and the caste formalities of dress were strictly enjoined on the sculptor. The *tunic* was

[1] Wells figures are illustrated, S. Gardner, Pls. CXL, CXLI, CXLII.

garment for all; but the monk had his cowl, the noble his smock or *surcoat*, the ecclesiastic his vestment, the knight his mail, the artisan his leather jacket—all of fixed regulated habit. So each being dressed for his degree and station was unconscious of occasion for fashion. Thus, while the thirteenth-century sculptor obtained the skill to render particulars of drapery and armour, and did so with increasing minuteness, yet from 1200 to 1300 his works cannot be dated to decade or even half-century by costume.

But this ceases towards the end of the century. "Countess Aveline" at Westminster declares her date as *c.* 1290, because with her a particular rendering of drapery[1] has come into the intention of the *imaginator*, and this because his art, like the dress itself, has grown personal and interests itself in individuality. Costume was so fashionably indicative of sex and its departure from earlier vocational habit was advancing to a place in the sun. The *mode* was the badge of rank as its first art of social luxury; century by century it has since been enlarging its net, and now bids fair to compass the whole globe with uniform indistinction[2]. But in the fourteenth century its appearance on a sculptor's effigy had this indication, that with him it was a surrender of the religious outlook upon Art. Aristocratic personality took the place of religious sanctity beside the altar, and thereafter monuments, brasses, and memorial stones were no more than the fashion gazettes of the heavenly mansions.

(*c*) Fashion in the Fourteenth-century Effigy

Still the medieval artist worked in terms of reality: so when the "Ecclesiastic" on his late thirteenth-century tomb is carved, not in linen vestments, as heretofore, but habited in silk draperies,

[1] See author's *Med. Fig.-Sculp. in Eng.* p. 345, also pp. 347, 349.

[2] All races and conditions seek now to clothe themselves democratically and uniformly—to be *moded* in the future, no doubt, by decree of the League of Nations.

we note that they were a new luxury, become current in ecclesiastical circles[1]. So for the "Knight," if his marble, stone or wood presentment *c.* 1300 has over its mail the linen *surcoat* we know him of Edward I's knight errantry. But after 1310, the sculptor of Westminster begins to carve him with an embroidered and petticoated jacket of silk, called technically *cyclas*, a bit of finery with a skirted tail. In another twenty years or so the jacket has lost its skirt, and become a close fitted *jupon* (or jumper we may call it) heraldically coloured[2]. At this date too the memorial "Lady" has discarded the girdled tunic, for a gown fitted to her waist, the introductory step to all the successive fashions of petticoat display[3].

But in them all the sculptor's progressions of drapery were in no sense fancy costumings such as are practised in artists' studios—they were not riggings out of a lay figure. Ideal costume even for the "Madonna" or the "Christ" was outside his conception because his innocence of eye accepted current costume with no *arrière pensée* for its artistic improvement[4]. In the fourteenth century the *imaginator* took men and women as they walked abroad—part of the pageant of things that was the necessary ground of their representation. Accordingly when he conceived his knight-effigy with legs crossed, it was the observed attitude of natural recumbency[5]. Mail allowed free movement, so knights in chain armour could lie in easy attitude. But *c.* 1320 plate armour was added to mail—steel-pieces being attached as defences against the lance that was the weapon in tourney displays. Then, since the protection-leggings of leather or steel

[1] "Ecclesiastics" of successive dates are illustrated in author's *Med. Fig.-Sculp. in Eng.* pp. 604, 605, 620, 639.

[2] "Knights," *Ibid.* pp. 588, 607, 654, 680.

[3] "Ladies," *Ibid.* pp. 349, 691.

[4] "Madonna," *Ibid.* pp. 321, 330, 357, 440.

[5] The *Crusader* theory, like the *Freemason*, seems one of those perennial fallacies, that weeding out never seems to extirpate. *Ibid.* pp. 602, 611.

cumbered the legs, to cross them was no easy attitude of repose: the knight-effigy accordingly rises on his side as a warrior ready to leap to his feet[1]. From 1360 onward, when cover plates were attached to joints, the knight at arms is stiffened from head to foot, and the monument-maker had perforce to straighten out the recumbent figure. There would be a practical absurdity in showing him all spikes and angles, in any *négligé* attitude[2]. So if the imager, turning memorialist, lost his earlier capacity for monumental sculpture, yet in the fourteenth century he was as close to the romantic fact as his predecessor, the thirteenth-century mason-sculptor, had been to the constructive need. Still as costumiers, rather than as portrait artists, the later effigyists studied their figures[3].

(*d*) Decorated Motives of Romance

The sepulchral representations well illustrate the varieties of craft and material as well of costume that shop-sculpture introduced. For example, the brass memorial of Sir Hugh Hastings at Elsing, Norfolk, is engraved with his figure and that of his various royal and noble relations habited in the dress of courtiers[4]. They have the showy accessories of knightly armour and heraldic display: we may see the colour of such a pageantry in manuscript-illumination like that called the Luttrell Psalter[5]. Of the same costuming are portrait-paintings at Westminster

[1] *Ibid.* pp. 597, 649, 650. [2] *Ibid.* pp. 680, 788.

[3] *Ibid.* pp. 673 seq. Only in the case of kings can any notion of portraiture be read into the memorialist sculpture of the Middle Ages. The point is fully discussed in the references given.

[4] The memorial "brasses" give examples of medieval costume that can be accurately dated. See H. Druitt, *Costume in Brasses*, pp. 154 seq. Flemish *provenance* for the Elsing brass seems doubtful in view of the architectural details of the engraved canopy which are those of the Westminster monuments—forms unknown abroad. See P. Biver, *Bulletin Monumental*, 1909.

[5] Now in the British Museum, but illustration from it is not at present to be got from the authorities.

Abbey on *Sedilia* which are early in the fourteenth century. The portrait of Richard II in the Jerusalem chamber, *c.* 1390, is of similar art in its personal distinction and rich robing. And just so the Decorated artist would robe churches in costume, arraying the masoned surfaces in gold and green, red and blue. So too the glass of fourteenth-century windows echoed the gala dress of nobles and ladies, in concerted brilliancies of living light[1].

The most of the fourteenth-century glass is gone from the windows of our churches, and the colours have perished from their stone surfaces: we have more certainly and in greater quantity the sculpture pieces expressing this aristocratic era of English art. We can see how the "Madonna" was imaged, as a Queen at York, *c.* 1310, with the sway of the figure that was the courtly fashion[2]. So the royal line of saintship figured as Kings and Knights on the west front of Exeter, seated as if at a coronation festival. The heavenly host of Angels are at Exeter as a minstrel band in attendance, like appointed officials at a lordly ceremonial[3]. The renunciation of earthly things had little meaning for the fourteenth-century carver: jesters and mummers[4] were as often his theme in church-work as any saintly character. Dogma had to yield place to pride of life as well as to luxury of art, when masons' heraldry was everywhere—in carved mimicry of war's array or in the lists of tourney. The uniform of lordship now appears in the decorative use of the battlement enrichment in architecture. In Hall and Bower the storming of the castle of Love, held by ladies, had been a popular pageant theme, and keyed to the tone of chanson and novello was the knight's tomb

[1] There are some good coloured illustrations of English glass from drawings by L. R. Saint in Hugh Arnold, *Stained Glass*, pp. 92, 96, 104, 108, 112, 120, 124—mostly from York Minster.

[2] A French fashion: see author's *Med. Fig.-Sculp. in Eng.* p. 330. As at Wells the figuring may also indicate Christ's royal ancestry.

[3] *Ibid.* p. 351.

[4] *Ibid.* pp. 342, 387.

worked with little battlements as of a mimic castle[1]. Indeed by the end of the fourteenth century the battlemented parapet had enlarged itself and grew so much the commonplace frilling of a church, that we accept it as appropriate[2]. But in the fourteenth century the castle motive coincided with the actual crenellation of manor-houses. Many hundreds of lords and squires obtained leave to *crenellate* in the reigns of Edward II and Edward III, and as we have said monastic houses sought this privilege of lordship, had knights in fee, and gatehouses ornamented with knightly shields[3].

N. THE SOCIAL EVOLUTION

(*a*) Citizen Church-building. (*b*) The Mason as a Specialist. (*c*) Decorated Traceries and Vaults. (*d*) The Building Disability for Sculpture. (*e*) Chantry Habit and the Gloucester Masoncraft.

(*a*) Citizen Church-building

We can say then that the first period of romantic art passed into the second under circumstances in which knightly courage and then martial energy created the dominant expression of fourteenth-century life. Edward I had been an English King; but Edward III aspired to be a European conqueror, and his claim to the French crown initiated a century of warfare. Materially it meant a diversion abroad of English interests and

[1] See illustration of carved ivory, G. G. Coulton, *Med. Garner*, p. 269. The Chertsey Abbey picture tiles, *c.* 1300, show the same mimic battlement. See author's *Med. Art in Eng.* p. 363. In the Trumpington monument, Ely choir, and Prior Crauden's chapel its appearance as an architectural ornament would seem due to the masons of Ely Cathedral, *c.* 1325. See F. Bond, *Goth. Arch. in Eng.* p. 130.

[2] Tewkesbury Abbey, *c.* 1340, is an early example.

[3] York Nave, *c.* 1320. S. Gardner, Pl. LVII. Kirkham Gateway, author's *Goth. Art in Eng.* p. 334. The earliest angels as heralds, carrying shields, would seem on the soffits of the canopy over Richard II's tomb. See W. R. Lethaby, *Westminster Abbey and the King's Craftsmen*, pp. 279 seq.

resources, but it meant the passing of the era during which the building and adornment of royal and episcopal churches had absorbed English wealth. Incidentally it allowed the development of English civic institutions. If the elder aristocracies of religion and warfare were depleted, new classes were bred in their place, and thus the last two centuries of English medieval craftsmanship move in a different atmosphere from the first. The continental alliances, which Edward III's policy favoured, opened up the continent to English trade: Brittany and the Low Countries were brought into close connection with England. But when English towns began to expand, the crafts of luxury, that were heretofore of King and Court, found service in citizen display. Towns and villages were now the clients of the building art: great churches grew into being—in evidence neither of monastic nor official display, but as the pride of citizens. In the wealth of trade fourteenth-century parish-churches were as elaborately stone-dressed as had been the aristocratic quire-buildings: Winchelsea, Rye, Deal, are examples in the Channel seaports. St Mary Redcliffe among other churches in Bristol illustrates the commercial standing of the Avon port and its Mediterranean trade: Boston church that of the Wash and the Baltic: Newark speaks of Trent commerce: Hull, Patrington and St Mary's, Beverley, of the prosperity of the Humber trade[1]. In the Midlands there was a considerable fourteenth-century building of churches—in Oxfordshire, Northamptonshire, Lincolnshire and Cambridgeshire—from the wealth acquired in the exportations of wool which Edward III's continental policy made profitable. But when the building-mason thus came into the service of trading classes architectural expression immediately responded to the change.

[1] Illustrated, F. Bond, *Goth. Arch. in Eng.* St Mary Redcliffe, pp. 376, 525; Boston, p. 222; Patrington, *Eng. Church Arch.* p. 949.

(b) The Mason as a Specialist

Seeing that masons' superintendence had now become an aptitude of display, rather than of construction, the *magister* hawked his capabilities about the country. A good illustration is that of the tower and spire buildings at Lincoln and Salisbury, in 1307 and 1334 respectively[1]. The accounts of the latter tell us that its engineer was Richard of Farleigh: and moreover indicates him as engaged in other works at the same time at Bath and at Reading. But to raise a stone spire, the loftiest in England, upon the slender piers of the crossing that Robert the mason had provided in 1220 was an enterprise of some skill. A science of strengthening piers is to be recognized in the arches that Richard used for the purpose[2]. In fact he was a specialist, and these "straining" arches as they are called connect him with Wells where the fourteenth-century tower got a similar shoring of structural props. In fact the pride of the fourteenth century needed an engineering specialist who moreover was a consultant going from place to place to direct building operations. Robert of the thirteenth century had been part and parcel of his building job—living on it and on his death probably succeeded by his son or by another master mason appointed for the sole service of the work in hand: Richard of the fourteenth was an independent purveyor of his skills—like an imager irresponsible to locality for his craft or to material conditions for his art.

But a specialist mason has perforce to seek custom by attracting it, and so the constructive side of his aptitude tends to be secondary to the decorative. It was in accord with his times that fourteenth-century arches should commonly neglect the visible accents of stability, even coursing and wedge-shaping

[1] A contract made with Richard Gainsborough for work (1307) at Lincoln is in evidence and is thought to refer to the Cathedral Tower. See S. Gardner, Pl. XXVIII. Salisbury is shown, Pl. XXIX.

[2] See author's *Cath. Build.* pp. 21, 22. In the Fabric Rolls of Exeter are entries as to experts being called in *c.* 1320.

of the voussoirs which convey arch-scholarship to the eye. In their Gothic sensibility the arch-curves had sprung up to an emphasized point, as if lifting weight at the apex. Decorated style cultivates the piquancy of the apex being thrust up in what is called the *ogee*. Other fancy arch-forms too were used, sometimes straight-lined or polygonal and often with frilled cusps, that are frilled and cusped again[1]. Then too there was a merging of the arch into the simulacrum of the gable, that had once in the structural doorway or niche-head been actually the coping of roof over it. So conceived the "striding canopy" of the fourteenth century became the sign manual of an art that has left reality for display[2]. What had been the mechanics of structure were now dressed out as the puppets of a show—be-crocketed, be-canopied and be-traceried. And since material in this had now no conscience, these doll's-house mimicries could be executed in wood, marble, alabaster or metal[3].

(*c*) Decorated Traceries and Vaults

In its stone-craft practice Decorated tracery was very various and its patterns have been stock-in-trade for the designers of modern Gothic. But in the fourteenth century they were not patterns but the exuberant workmanship of local quarry-crafts. Thus north English masonry spread its window-head into the

[1] S. Gardner, Pls. CXXX, CXXXI, CXXXII.

[2] See author's *Med. Art in Eng.* Chap. IX, with many illustrations.

[3] Examples of false architectural ornament are shown in S. Gardner's plates of Decorated and Perpendicular—e.g. Pls. LXXII, CLXI, CLXII, CLXIII. At Winchester the oak stalls of 1300 started a whole series of tabernacle works in mimicry of stone, the Bishop's canopy at Exeter being somewhat later. Metal work with this detail is frequent in croziers and other minute uses. A large late example of metal "tracery" is that of the screen-work enclosing Henry VII's tomb in Westminster. For the alabaster traceries see author's *Med. Fig.-Sculp. in Eng.* pp. 500, 501. The glass-painter's use of the tabernacle with its curious craze for architectural semblance has bred in modern glass some absurd *antics*.

Plate VI

BISHOP GRANDISSON'S IVORY (British Museum)

Plate VII

ALABASTER RETABLE (Victoria and Albert Museum)

convolutions of a branching, almost twining, vine. Further south flowing lines were of less vegetable suggestion, and the Midland churches used what is called *reticulated* tracery in even spacings of trefoils or lozenges. The earlier arch-forms of window construction survive to mix with the flowing patterns in East England. But it is notable that when spaces open out in the window-heads—as in *Kentish* tracery[1], the craft of glass-painting is seeking panels for its picture displays. Moreover in all this play of ornamental device the mason was becoming subservient to the decorator: for the fourteenth-century window was showing itself a mason's dexterity rather than building expediency. But still the Decorated varieties of tracery were no futile exercises of an architect's drawing-board—in the fourteenth century they were, as we may call it, Craftsman's Romance.

The fourteenth-century vault too had as much variety and indulgence of romantic masoncraft, in which the structural conscience gradually yielded to prevarication of Gothic truth. The English vaulting system, in distinction from the French, had multiplied ribs in the constructive expediency of the level-crowned vault; then for the chapter-house[2] the masons found they could vault an oblong without a central pillar. But this engineering feat could only be consummated by the device of using ribs as show pieces, the real work lying in the surface of the ceiling itself, pieced together to form a single coherence. When the stability of a vault was so engineered, the ribs remained as ornamental survivals of what had been Gothic construction. Conceived originally as building they were now patterning,

[1] See S. Gardner, Pls. CI, CII, CIII, CIV; also T. G. Jackson, *Goth. Arch.* Vol. II. pp. 55—64.

[2] See author's *Cath. Build.* Pl. 14. Dispensing with a central pillar, with the ribs radiating from it, the mason had an octagonal opening, into which a more or less flat stone ceiling could be fitted and be stable. The idea was tried in the Southwell chapter-house and then translated into the covering of an oblong hall like Gloucester quire.

cusped and grouped in radiating panels as in a window. In Gloucester quire[1] the ceiling has become in fact a cover of concrete—the aggregate of it not formless pebbles but a devised mesh of shaped and fitted stone. Then the arch-ribs, curving upwards uniformly from each springing in the craft of the Gloucester mason, *c.* 1348, become what are called *fans*[2], in fact an ornamental corbel.

(*d*) The Building Disability for Sculpture

Yet if masons' device was so exercised in the church fabric itself, there was being lost that which had been its building right hitherto, the sense of figure-sculpture. The arcadings of the Ely Lady-chapel, and the stone sedilia of Exeter presbytery and Tewkesbury[3] show diversions from expressive to mechanical sculpture. It is not the imager, but the entailer (*intagliator*) who at Ely[4] tells the story of the Virgin. His interest in the matter is its decorative combination with the bulging canopy-work. Fourteenth-century figure-composition was usually content with mere rivalry with leaf crockets and pinnacles. If Exeter front, like Christchurch reredos, is a wonder of rich surfacing, in which expressive figure-work has its part[5], on the quire-screen at Exeter were small images and panels in carved relief, flat and richly painted[6]. The trades of church masoncraft were falling apart. The image-sculptor had retreated to his shop : the building sculptor expended his art on the niche that was a mere frame filled afterwards by the imaging function. And indeed the building art was ready to conceive of a niche without a figure, with the same detachment as the imager could specialize his image, as outside any architectural setting.

[1] *Ibid.* Pl. 22. [2] As in the cloister, *Ibid.* Pl. 23.

[3] A good example at Wells is shown, S. Gardner, Pl. LVIII.

[4] *Ibid.* Pl. CXXXV. [5] See author's *Med. Fig.-Sculp. in Eng.* pp. 47, 351.

[6] S. Gardner, Pl. LVI. See *Exeter Fabric Rolls*, A. H. Thompson, for the years 1320 and onwards : the present paintings are Jacobean.

As the rupture widened, they were architectural settings too that the monument maker supplied. The shopcrafts of sculpture were advancing on the architectural position all along the line. London, as we have seen, in 1300 had its specialist camp of guild-building[1]. It had too a flourishing commerce in effigies whose conveyance to all the kingdom is attested by the similar makes in wood, stone and alabaster in different parts of England[2]. We see too that the gabled tombs and canopies that were of Westminster origin appear in the provinces[3]. Marble furnitures like the shrine at St Albans would seem also a craft of London monument makers whose use of the Dorset stone had been a long tradition[4]. A little later we find alabaster from Derbyshire brought to London and used with the Purbeck marble, making composite monuments such as Edward II's monument at Gloucester[5]. These elaborate monuments of English make came to be of continental repute also: we read of instances of their exportation, as, for example, London craftsmen are given licence for the tomb of John, Duke of Brittany to be taken to Nantes. But if in such productions fashion, caprice, and the reputation of aristocratic patronage dominated expression, building craft, as in London so elsewhere, was become not a builder's utility but a special expertness of craft device. As the monopolies of the imager and the monumental effigy-maker were established, so the building scheme developed as the trick of a trade: its detail was supplied from a Gloucester shop to the memorial chantries of Tewkesbury[6] and soon Gloucester quire itself could be built as a superabundant piece of chantry luxury.

[1] See back p. 86.

[2] See author's *Med. Fig.-Sculp. in Eng.* pp. 666 seq., 673 seq.

[3] As at Canterbury and Winchelsea (see Blore, *Monumental Remains*, No. 6); F. H. Crossley, *English Church Monuments*, has photographs of many of these gable-tombs.

[4] S. Gardner, Pl. CLXI.

[5] On a Purbeck marble base, is an alabaster effigy, the canopy over being in freestone. See author's *Med. Fig.-Sculp. in Eng.* p. 673.

[6] S. Gardner, Pl. CLIX. For English Chantries see Count Paul Biver, *Bulletin Monumental*, 1908.

(*e*) Chantry Habit and the Gloucester Masoncraft

Throughout England the established crafts of church structure found patrons in the squires and small landowners who were growing rich by the sale of English wool. In the fashion of the time they spent money in founding memorial chantries. In the building and adornment of such chapels guilds of furnishing masons would seem to have come into existence in most cities during the fourteenth century, getting custom alongside the imagers and goldsmiths whose headquarters were at Westminster and London, with kings as their patrons. The whole conduct of the architectural enterprise was altering by the middle of the century in that these provincial trade-crafts, that had access to immediate quarries of stone suitable for decorative shaping, created special types of church furniture. At Exeter, Bristol, Gloucester, Nottingham, Lincoln, York, we have before the Black Death mason-shops developing trade activities, and supplying sepulchral monuments, quire-screens, etc., in many varieties of fanciful extravagance. Yet the disappearance of structural substance had been all along a gradual movement: begun in the thirteenth century, it was not to be full master of architectural effect for another hundred years. Its action on church-building proper was initiated as early as 1310 at Bristol in the skeleton treatments of construction. Then in Wells quire the method has advanced to a network veneer of panellings repeating themselves over building surfaces—over windows and walls, over piers and ceilings—knitting them together in a coherent ordered intricacy with simulated fineness[1].

What the Somerset and Gloucester masons practised grew to make the manner of later Gothic. Though abandoning all that sense of sculptural expression which had been the Gothic prerogative, it was an expert one in its own line. By its repetitions of shafts and cusped arches—by its slenderly cut mouldings and conventionalized curvatures—by its shallow enrichments

[1] See for illustrations F. Bond, *Gothic Arch. in Eng.* p. 127.

of textures—by its square cut bosses and crockets, it was an economical dexterity of building craft. The cusped panelling of the Gloucester mason was a ready and cheap enrichment under cover of which clumsy solidities could be disguised. The regularity of the method, and the standardized areas it afforded, were of practical intention as allowing an organized decoration by the special crafts that fourteenth-century luxury had brought into being. Whereas the early romantic "Decorated" with its fancy shapings and curvatures meant irregular interspacings in wall and window, whose treatment by sculptor or glass-painter could only be that of an artist working on the building, the Gloucester panel method standardized oblongs[1], into which were set the figure-works of the *imaginator* working away from the building in his shop. It was a business proposition to the painter of saint figures, or to the statuary of saint images, that the structure could be built for him ready for his subjects. But the tale of fourteenth-century Romance had been told: its book was closed.

[1] See author's *Cath. Build.* Pl. 22; also T. G. Jackson, *Goth. Arch.* Vol. II. pp. 94, 101, 103.

CHAPTER VIII

THE LATEST GOTHIC, 1350—1540

O. AFTER THE BLACK DEATH

(*a*) The Break of Architectural Style. (*b*) The Official Perpendicular. (*c*) The Black Death and the Monkish Orders. (*d*) The Decline of the Monastic Institution. (*e*) Church Expressions—Old and New. (*f*) Friars and People.

(*a*) The Break of Architectural Style

The conditions immediately following on the Black Death cannot be easily gathered from the records we have of cathedral and abbey church-building. The plague mortality was, we know, enormous and, it is calculated, reduced by more than half the population of England, and in the paralysis of social activity which ensued building enterprise would be closed down[1]. Yet the building accounts that have come down to us do not give prominent instances. At Westminster there is no special break in the fabric rolls—masons were employed from 1350 to 1360 much as they had been in the decade before and after. At York it is not easy to find evidence that there was any marked discontinuance of the rebuilding scheme—the nave was given its vault in 1354 and the quire proceeded forthwith. At Exeter[2], Ely and Winchester workmen were still on the cathedral fabrics in 1355: and at Gloucester especially the elaborate transformations of the Romanesque fabric were pressed on without any slackening —cloister and quire were carried to completion. No doubt in estimating such records allowance must be made for the vagueness of cathedral and monastic chronicles which assign buildings to periods of office, attributing them to such and such a Bishop,

[1] Cunningham, *Eng. Ind. and Com.* pp. 332, 333.

[2] Good evidence is in the Exeter Fabric Rolls.

Abbot or Prior, who may, like Bishop Hatfield of Durham[1], have lived through the whole period of the pestilences—in his case the work to which his name is attached was of two periods some forty years apart. Moreover we may somewhat discount the particular instances above, for the building works at Westminster and York were special cases in great cities, where though the population might be reduced, the building trades would not be likely to be entirely wiped out. The residue of craftsmen would be specially commandeered for royal works or those of official standing: and in the case of Gloucester, we know it as the seat of the Court on many occasions during the pestilence years—for example Parliament sat in the Guest-house 1378. On the other hand if we look up and down England, to the general body of cathedrals and churches that were building extensively before 1350, no new works are indicated for the fifteen years of plague prevalence. Then for another fifteen building is resumed with almost pre-pestilence diligence. But then the character of the new work is significant: at Gloucester there is sequence of craftsmanship, but elsewhere in England it is as if the thread of style had been abruptly broken. The quarry dexterities, that in the first half of the fourteenth century had given such variety and vitality to the luxury trades of church-building, have disappeared. In their place have come set manners of masons' design, an expert accomplishment it is true, but formalized—so we see at Winchester, Canterbury, York and Chichester[2]. The new aspects are those of a regulated and carefully distributed activity of masons' craft, uniform throughout England: and moreover

[1] See E. Blore, *Monumental Remains*, No. 14. Bishop Hatfield held the see 1345—1381. His throne in the quire was a stone erection afterwards used as his monument, its base is in the florid manner of the York decoration of 1340, its canopy has all the dexterous Gloucester device of Perpendicular furniture.

[2] Beverley Minster Front and Norwich Quire clerestory are also reckoned as *c.* 1380: the Norwich vaults were nearly 100 years later.

it is what the Gloucester masons had used for their abbey-building[1], and so was it to be unchanged for the next hundred years. Perpendicular has some right to be called an *order* of "English Gothic" as we speak of a "Roman Doric"—William of Wykeham might have been the Vitruvius, who ordered and systematized its formulae of style.

(*b*) The Official Perpendicular

For the century and half, during which English masons wrought latest Gothic, our church-building has a very distinct insularity. The continental building forms, though moving in the spheres of the respective nationalities of Flanders, France, Germany and Spain much as we recognize to-day, were expressions on a common basis of style in that they used broad building masses, which were overlaid by laceworks of intricate architectural device. But in England the architectural device was of itself solid essential construction, and kept for the whole period the aspect of a methodical and recognized stability. A Perpendicular building explains itself to the eye as an ingenious but perfectly successful achievement of builders' engineering. Whereas Gothic masoncraft had been practically of one breed up to the fourteenth century, by the end of it English and Continental church-building cannot be confused—they have developed forms of different mentality[2].

The first phase of the English speciality was found in the official dragooning of the building crafts that followed on the

[1] See author's *Cath. Build.* Pl. 25 as to Winchester and references already given as to Gloucester. The east end of York Minster is in S. Gardner, Pl. CVI. The regulations governing the master mason and his *socii* at York in 1370 is in G. G. Coulton, *Social Life in Britain*, p. 489. In author's *Cath. Build.* pp. 82 seq. the points are fully discussed; somewhat similar views are taken by T. G. Jackson, *Goth. Arch.* 1915, Vol. II. Chap. XX.

[2] T. G. Jackson, *Goth. Arch.* Vol. II gives three illustrations useful for comparison, Florence p. 224, Candebec p. 151 and Gloucester p. 94.

Black Death. The Westminster records show masons of Gloucester in London all through the fourteenth century[1]. Now it was in Gloucester monument-making (see back p. 115) that the qualities of Perpendicular were developed—discovering dexterity in what was in fact an architectural decrepitude. It is curious that as such they should be not only coincident with the birth of English literature, but that our poet Chaucer himself held the post of King's Surveyor and so was concerned in the establishment of the Gloucester régime.

In the Plague years from 1350 to 1370 church-building must have ceased as a social activity. Not only would the pestilences have taken heavy toll of the building agents, but the survivors under the stress of labour deficiency were called up for agriculture and put on the land. However, Gloucester craftsmanship was, we have said, not completely disorganized. The plagues were capricious in their visitation: Gloucester possibly escaped the worst mortality, since the Parliament seems to have met there on several years from 1350 onwards. For recovery of English social life *Labour* legislation was brought into force: acts were passed regulating expenses and controlling wages. Moreover King's officers commandeered building-masons from all the country for the King's work, and for the last half of the fourteenth century the King's department of works was one which King's officers, like William of Wykeham and Chaucer, administered. Now since the Gloucester habit of panelled construction was, in its system of essential economy, capable of formalized application to extensive works, it was adapted for a bureaucratic conduct of building: it may be compared indeed to the stereotyped architecture of Imperial Rome. Like that it could take similar terms for the whole kingdom; like that, too, be practically without development, or change of expression for long periods. At any rate the uniformity

[1] W. R. Lethaby, *Westminster Abbey and the King's Craftsmen.*

or standard fixity of the official Perpendicular during a hundred and fifty years is remarkable after the continual movement and constant variety of the previous Gothic. And as the constructive art, so was the decorative: its painting, its sculpture and its glass, its wood and metal craftsmanship standardize their expressions. In a broad sense the general revolution of fifteenth-century society fostered the merely decorative and unsculptural expression of the Gloucester masoncraft, so that it framed an imagery and a glass painting formal and uninspired beside the expressions of the earlier Romance[1].

(*c*) The Black Death and the Monkish Orders

In this decline of art-feeling, which was significant of the latest period of English Gothic, the factor of monastic decay shows itself immediately the most important of the results of the Black Death. The exalted place, that the early fourteenth-century monasteries held as aristocratic preserves, was secure while their guest-houses were fashionable, while Episcopal halls were the home of court ceremony and Chapters had official dignities. The cleric had long been the principal landholder of the realm, and to the various orders of ecclesiastic function belonged all learning and profession. But except in the case of certain ascetics, such as the Carthusians, the monastic disciplines had faded into a general habit of well-being and social consequence as of lords of the soil. Benedictines, Cluniacs, Cistercians, Augustinian, and other Canons, whose various rules meant much for the earlier phases of English art[2], now held regulations

[1] The wonderful dexterity of draughtsmanship obtained in the English crafts of glass painting is well shown in the drawings by L. B. Saint, H. Arnold, *Stained Glass*, Pls. 34—44. A similar efficiency of masoncraft was that of Gloucester and it was capable of reproduction. Whereas in the case of *Norman*, *Early English* or *Decorated*, replicas fail and imitations are necessarily heartless and tasteless, *Perpendicular* can be less offensively "restored," for though manufactured, its mechanism can be appreciated.

[2] A. H. Thompson, *English Monasteries*, pp. 25 seq.

very much alike. Bishops, Abbots and Priors of all the Orders were associates of princes, lords and knights. Secular and Regular Canons, monks and friars were propertied classes, maintaining their possessions and exercising feudal powers. For example, at the time of the Black Death Bishop Wyvil of Salisbury, remarkable, so we read, neither in person nor in character, fortified the seven chief manors of his see, and his memorial brass in the Cathedral shows him as lord in his castle of Old Sarum, with a warrior at the door as guardian of his feif[1]. Such assertions of lordship, as the fourteenth-century gateways of monasteries had made customary, were in building at Thornton, Ely and Battle Abbey on into the fifteenth century. But if abbots and priors could be extravagant in guest-parlours and manor-houses they were seldom enterprised to build quires. For in spite of conventual estates and revenues credit for building was ceasing to be of monastic ambition: the decay was there that in another one hundred and eighty years was to become a mortal malady: to its dissolution was hastening the medieval era of church-art in England[2].

(*d*) The Decline of the Monastic Institution

As regards monasteries the immediate and lasting effect had been the depletion of the monastic *personnel*. It is said that many of the smaller houses were wiped out of existence by the Black Death: all had such decreases that the corporate continuity, that was the essence of conventual life, was broken. At Meaux, a Cistercian house in Yorkshire, out of forty-nine monks and conversi thirty-nine died in 1349. Another Cistercian house—that of Louth Park in Lincolnshire—with sixty-six monks in 1300, had only ten inmates at the Dissolution[3]. The effect of

[1] See author's *Goth. Art in Eng.* p. 384 for illustration.

[2] The first half of the sixteenth century was in France a building era, in which (see back pp. 89 seq.) the great cathedrals of the thirteenth century were completed. In England except in royal building and the chantries of bishops there is little of consequence, see however p. 133 below.

[3] A. H. Thompson, *English Monasteries*, p. 33.

the plague was in fact decline of both discipline and repute. The monasteries and canons'-houses, in the dearth of aristocratic support, had to admit a lower social grade and a coarser practice of rule. In this connection we read of certain efforts by the state to rehabilitate monastic institutions as centres of social and religious orthodoxy—for example, Henry V's foundation of the Bridgetine Nuns at Sion in Middlesex, and the Carthusian house at Shene—a royal foundation in 1414. But as a power in fifteenth-century architecture, such foundations were negligible. It is true that some monastic houses were building up to 1400, and some additions to both monks' and canons' churches were undertaken in the fifteenth, but the character of these later enterprises is significant, they are of parish-church expression[1]. The art instinct was no longer sensitive to the monastic stimulus and in its place was come another sense of religious duty.

(*e*) Church Expressions—Old and New

In original accomplishment the vast fabric of the medieval church had met the needs of medieval society, and all through the thirteenth century the English Cathedral had served as the national assembly place for all classes under the established religious system. Its accommodations were based on institutions that were popular, and reflected the life and thought of all. The shrine and its pilgrims, the chapel and its votaries were the accepted facts of the social system in which Gothic art moved. But as the church of the later fourteenth century grew indifferent to these earlier enthusiasms other needs displaced them. Colleges

[1] Sherborne Abbey is after Gloucester the most conspicuous work of Benedictine rebuilding in the fifteenth century. The special circumstances of a fire, after a riot, enabled the monks to mulct the citizens for the costs. See author's *Cath. Build.* Pl. 28, for Constable's drawing: see F. Bond, *Eng. Church Arch.* p. 361 for fan vault. At Norwich and Oxford, St Frideswide's were abbey-church vault renewals. At Bath Abbey was a rebuilding in the early sixteenth century of the Romanesque church.

and school-houses became ecclesiastic foundations, and their buildings were for learning rather than for relics and miracles.

Already before 1400 the new and the old forces were being marshalled—the religious position having its two camps. On the one side were the Wickliffites, to whom the dynastic support of the House of Lancaster was being given : on the other was the elder régime to which adhered the clerical supremacies that the heresies threatened. Political suppressions intervened and in the rivalry of the two Houses, that of York appeared as the patron of religious legitimacy and for the time Lollards were state-suppressed. So for the fifteenth century, at least, the orthodox position held its ground[1], the Friars being the standing army of the faith entrenched behind the usages and expressions of a thousand years. Yet not for either monk, king, noble or friar was now the determination or the government of art-progress.

(*f*) Friars and People

The Friar orders had been founded in the thirteenth century, but none of their buildings of that century in England—with the exception perhaps of the Franciscan church in London favoured by Queen Eleanor[2]—could be influential for architecture. In the first half of the fourteenth century the churches built for Franciscan, for Dominican or for Austin Friar services had their ritual expression in a long unaisled chancel with a narrow entry under a bell-tower. But also the broad-aisled naves, as large audience halls in which crowds could hear the eloquence of the preacher, make in many continental cities a distinct variety of church-building. In England however there seems to have been nothing of this scale or kind, for our largest Friars' preaching-naves, such as those of London, were as the naves of parish churches. Still the fifteenth-century expression

[1] G. G. Coulton, *Social Life in Britain*, should be consulted.

[2] Grey Friars, 300 feet long, 95 feet wide, and 64 feet high, it was the largest church built for Friars in England : only the marble pavings now remain.

of an open church was the Friar-type, represented in our towns although the Friar buildings have themselves now almost entirely disappeared. Are we then to associate the diffusion of Gloucester masoncraft with Friars' economy of church-building and so derive Perpendicular? Aisled naves—open halls with slender arcades, broad windows and a fine economical use of stone—such had been in building throughout the length and breadth of Europe since the earliest essays of Gothic style. To them the Gloucester mason had given his practical and efficient craft at the close of the fourteenth century, so that even for cathedral- and abbey-churches *parish-church* naves, as we may call them, were built as at Winchester and Canterbury. It would seem then that broad open church-building had its wide use of Gloucester masoncrafts, not because the Friars disseminated it, but because it was parish-church use[1].

The point is interesting, as explaining the position of medieval art in 1350 and the following years. The monastic ideal as the pioneer of medieval civilization was accepted in the twelfth and thirteenth centuries as the nurse of a special piety and special learning: but in the early fourteenth century membership of a great monastery became less a religious than a social privilege as of an aristocratic club to-day. After the Black Death, while conventual discipline was failing, social distinction left the monk, but still the monastic revenues and privileges were in evidence; and in towns envy was excited against luxuries and assertions that no longer commanded respect. Fifteenth-century literature is full of criticisms of the religious, and passed into invective specially levelled at the Friars[2]. Indeed the closings of religious houses and diversions of their endowments to colleges and schools had been going on spasmodically for some hundred years before Henry VIII dissolved and confiscated.

[1] For Canterbury Nave see F. Bond, *Eng. Ch. Arch.* p. 572; for Lavenham, S. Gardner, Pl. LXI.

[2] Jusserand, *English Wayfaring Life*, pp. 298 seq.

P. POPULAR ARCHITECTURE

(*a*) Colleges and Mass Priests. (*b*) Guild chapels and Parish Churches. (*c*) Democracy in Towers, Porches, etc. (*d*) The Shop-art of Church-furnishing. (*e*) Bourgeois Sculpture. (*f*) The Trades of Altar, Shrine, and Church-service. (*g*) End of Church-building.

(*a*) Colleges and Mass Priests

It came so that in the Collegiate establishments was the latest English development of building art, and this with two sides—(1) the Perpendicular of State building of the People, (2) the Parish-church Art. The official organization of masons' labour comes before us magnificently in the work of the royal officers, at New College, Oxford, at Winchester, at Windsor, and King's College, Cambridge[1]. But by its side more continuously and for the whole of the hundred and fifty years was a less official and more democratic use of Perpendicular style, that up and down the country-side found its occasions in lesser collegiate building and in the chantry aisles and chapels of parish-churches. In the fourteenth and fifteenth centuries clerics in various associations were attached to churches, and for them, and for their services, were built chancels fitted with stalls. The dissolution of the monasteries and the suppression of chantries and guilds that came in 1536 and the following years did not generally affect the fabrics of collegiate foundations; many of them remain to this day in public use, and some of our best later medieval building is to be seen at Stratford-on-Avon, Coventry, Manchester and Newcastle, large churches with long chancels and broad-aisled naves—in one sense of style with that of Cathedrals and Abbeys and of scarcely less scale and dignity[2].

[1] New College, 1380; Winchester College, 1387; Winchester Cathedral Nave, 1394, see S. Gardner, Pl. LIX; Windsor, Eton College, 1441; Cambridge, King's College, begun 1446, see T. G. Jackson, *Goth. Arch.* Vol. II. p. 110; Windsor, St George's Chapel, begun 1473, see S. Gardner, Pl. LXII—a whole century of stereotyped official style.

[2] In cathedral- as well as in abbey-churches were examples of the current popular masoncraft, see Canterbury Nave, 1380, Lavenham, *c.* 1450,

The official organization established building-masons as a privileged class[1], that took service with king, commoner, or corporation. For each city were its shops of decorative church-furniture, as in the fourteenth century, the patrons of the arts being all orders and all classes. Moreover each country-side had its quarry-centre of craft, which supplied windows and doorways, panels and pinnacles ready worked. But in it all architectural device remained mainly what the requirements of the greater building had formalized—Parish-church art adapted and arranged but did not initiate motives.

After England recovered from the plague of the Black Death, a period of prosperity ensued[2], when France that had hitherto been the wealthy country of West Europe fell from this position. After 1350 the devastations of the hundred years' war visited most of its area: Flanders and England prospered in its stead—Flanders as the manufacturing country, England as the producer of the staple wool. When at the end of the fourteenth century England herself began to manufacture, trade populations grew prosperous all over the country. There was initiated a building of Parish-churches with the moneys that, whether of family or guild accumulation, were in substance the profits of successful trade[3].

(*b*) Guild Chapels and Parish Churches

Such were the interests concerned in the bulk of building. Grading down from the royal foundations came all degrees of collegiate bodies whose office was an extension of chantry

Pl. LXI, and Ripon Nave, *c.* 1500. At Oxford the Abbey-quire and the Divinity Schools (Pl. LXVI) have the forms of vault scarcely varied.

[1] See author's *Cath. Build.* pp. 87 seq.

[2] Cunningham, *Eng. Ind. and Com.* pp. 372 seq. where the evolution of modern conditions is discussed, the development of trade and the readjustment of social activities in the Lancaster and York period had its ups and downs.

[3] Lavenham, S. Gardner, Pl. LXI; Southwold, *Ibid.* Pl. XV; Boston, *Ibid.* Pl. XXXI; Terrington, St Clement's, *Ibid.* Fig. 12.

ritual. We find mass-priests endowed for memorial service, and often also functioned for education[1]. There was too a great growth of religious Guilds in all towns and villages throughout England, associations under neither obligation to monks nor high ecclesiastic, but with their own corporate organization. Such were expressly concerned in the building and adornment of parish-churches. When the drain of the French wars had depleted aristocratic resources, which were to be still further squandered in the dynastic wars of the king-makers, there came a bringing into prominence of new social distinction, and generally at the middle of the fifteenth century a wider wealth was expressed up and down in England in the country-side patronages of the church-building crafts.

One aspect of these arts grew up specially in the English habit of chapels, claimed as the property of families and served by private priests[2]. Church-planning developed as a series of enlargements and among these the guild chapel took its place in expression of the corporate life which the fifteenth and early sixteenth century was fostering in the cities. Trade-guilds and craft-guilds had origin in thirteenth-century city-life, but in the fifteenth they multiplied as religious clubs much on the lines of our Masons, Foresters, Good Templars and Burial Clubs. In one way or another the whole population was drawn into such associations. In the orthodox religious formula they were dedicated to a Saint, at whose altar in the parish-church the guild priest served, and whose feast-day was the annual gala —surviving sometimes to our day in the local fair-day. Guild chapels were sometimes outside the church fabric, but most often were part of its structure, built on as aisles and transepts, or sometimes initiating a complete rebuilding of the Parish-church.

[1] For school-house built over Lady-chapel at Christchurch, Hants. see author's *Goth. Art in Eng.* p. 438. A. Jessopp, *Great Pillage*, tells the story as to mass-priests' duty of schooling.

[2] A. H. Thompson, *Eng. Par. Ch.* pp. 121 seq.

The church fabric of the fifteenth century was extended in wide square-ended halls, each with its chantry or guild altar, enclosed in screen-work and decorated with the retables of the church furnishing trades that every town and country-side supplied[1].

The latest English style of Gothic, however much it might accept the religious tradition of display, had no sense of the earlier exclusiveness of a religious art. The skills of its building and decoration were those of trade interests—not of ecclesiastic intentions: Perpendicular enlargements of parish-churches were for mere area, not sanctity. They were built open from end to end in repudiation of the traditional *cross*-church tradition; and they had chancels projecting eastwards only where a full staff of clerics had to be seated. The typical English Parish-church has its aisles and arcades not as they had grown up in the Romanesque development of the constructional ritual of monastic building, but for the congregational convenience of obtaining for the mid-area the full light of aisle windowing. The parallel halls made one chamber visible from all points through open screen-divisions, behind which the appropriated chapels had each its altar[2].

In all this country-side building the crafts of woodwork grew into special consequence. The areas had to be ceiled for spans of from thirty to forty feet, and there grew up a skill and science of carpentry—exercised perhaps first in the Halls of Kings, but soon used for the scarcely less sumptuous roofings of the English Parish-church[3].

[1] Cirencester is a remarkable example. See F. Bond, *Goth. Arch.* p. 544.

[2] See Lynn, St Nicholas, S. Gardner, Pl. CV; Southwold, *Ibid.* Pl. XV, also F. Bond, *Eng. Church Arch.* p. 193; Wells, St Cuthbert's, p. 206; Norwich, St Stephen's, *Goth. Arch.* p. 228.

[3] See S. Gardner, Pls. LXIII, LXIV, LXV. For examples of the screen-works which were the speciality of the English wood-carver see S. Gardner, Pls. CLXIII, CLXIV; also F. Bond, *Screens and Galleries*, and *Wood-carvings in English Churches*.

(c) Democracy in Towers, Porches, etc.

Architecture was growing democratic in its exterior expressions also. The conspicuous example of latest English masonry in which a creative sense of Gothic construction appears is the English church-tower often standing square-topped with no visible pyramidal roofing or spire. The church of the fourteenth century had made the spire the crowning expression of Gothic romance in masoncraft, and up to 1350 one must believe that every Gothic tower was begun with the intention of a stone spire—or at all events that it proposed one of carpentry covered with lead[1]. Lightnings and conflagrations, winds and decays, were always bringing these wood spires to destruction, and the money to build a new one was not always forthcoming. So the habit of a square-topped, spireless tower became by custom agreeable to English eyes, and certainly after 1350 what with battlements and pinnacles or the occasional compromise represented by the octagonal or lantern "crown[2]," a truncated, flat-roofed bell-chamber was sufficient for its purpose. For in connection with churches bell-ringing was the popular sport, and so much was it honoured, that often the church tower is built for it, and on a scale to dwarf nave and chancel. Tower-building was in fact an exercise of popular religion in itself.

Conspicuous in this sense was the great bell-tower of Canterbury, square and spireless, a piece of parish-church masoncraft taken into cathedral service[3]. Significantly was it the last work of

[1] For fifteenth-century spires see St Mary Redcliffe, Bristol, S. Gardner, Fig. 45; Coventry, Fig. 46. For timber spires see F. Bond, *Eng. Ch. Arch.* pp. 925, 926.

[2] Boston, S. Gardner, Pl. XXXI; Newcastle, *Ibid.* Fig. 52. The bell-tower was not of ecclesiastic pretension. It was a civic dignity and its popular use was in secular institutions, such as bell-ringing guilds and church *ales*. The fifteenth-century bell-tower for Cathedrals has the same significance as the Market-cross of Winchester or Chichester, episcopal sops to civic democracy.

[3] *Ibid.* Pl. XXX.

English style in the finish of the premier Benedictine church, in whose structure both English Romanesque and English Gothic had at the bidding of Benedictine monks essayed their first notable works. It was as clear a case of surrender to the new politics as that of the bell-tower building of Cistercians and Augustinians in the last years of their existence. As institutions with funds threatened by Commissioners, the monastic houses sought to compound with the spoiler. So while he had the money to spend the Cistercian had his fling in a bell-tower as a sop to country-side sport just before the threatened revolution was to bring new owners into his property[1]. The latest monastic building was frankly domestic: these late Perpendicular towers (like the big porches that often accompanied them) were just stories of apartments—with square-headed windows for level ceilings[2]. Architecture was shaping its forms for manor-house building, and the church areas themselves had carpentry ceilings, flat and lead covered. In the cathedral nave of St Davids, no pretence of vault, nor memory of stone construction, survives in the dropping pendants of its beamed and panelled construction, like the tester of a bed[3]. The stone-aspiring experiment of Gothic had spent itself: Henry VIII was building Nonsuch and bringing Italian palace-deckers to England, to work in plaster and terracotta: so the brick towers of Essex, the porches of west-country churches and the beamed and boarded ceilings of the midlands could appropriately and with no change of feature have been those of manor-house building[4].

[1] As at Bolton, Furness and Fountains, S. Gardner, Pl. IV.

[2] See Burford, Pl. LXXXII; also F. Bond, *Eng. Church Arch.* pp. 724 seq.

[3] *Ibid.* p. 841.

[4] At Layer Marney, *c.* 1530, is a good example of a brick-built church and manor-house showing the new Italian terracotta ornaments; see F. Bond, *Eng. Church Arch.* p. 661. Also author's *Med. Fig.-Sculp. in Eng.* p. 719, for the church monument, whose effigy-figure has suggestions of the new sculpturesque as the first indication of the Renaissance.

(*d*) The Shop-art of Church-furnishing

During the whole of the fifteenth century the decking and furnishing of churches lay in the homely traditional trading of an established guild-commerce. Shopcraft and democratic sale in England could yield no religious or romantic nobility such as makes the charm of contemporary Renaissance work in Italy. It was not to be expected of our fifteenth century that the Florentine genius of any Donatello or della Robbia should enrich our art. Yet the imager's trade of the fifteenth century was an extensive one, and we have its examples come down to us in greater numbers and better preservation than what the earlier masons worked in the building stone of church structure. The altar-images of ivory, metal and wood have left scarcely a specimen, but there are some characteristic pieces in alabaster[1] and the figure-works set in screens or attached to tombs have escaped more often the general destruction. Indeed the late fourteenth- and fifteenth-century tomb-effigies can be studied in a continuous series. Though without the romantic dramatization of the earlier figures we find a sedate and ceremonial accomplishment in "knights" and "ladies," lying flat with folded hands. To the end is kept the character of a settled traditional art. The sculptor was occupied in the details of armour and costume[2] and his dexterity in the representations of these minutiae was a survival for tomb-sculpture beyond the Gothic period. But no breath of Italian *humanism* has flecked the level of English tradition: as secure as were the masons of King's College Chapel in their panelled conventions, so too were the alabaster workers of the memorial figure in their English trade—until the contemporary of Michael Angelo Torrigiano came to Westminster[3].

1 Some examples of images and statuettes are given in author's *Med. Fig.-Sculp. in Eng.* pp. 358 seq., also pp. 460 seq.

2 *Ibid.* Part III, Chaps. VI, VII.

3 *Ibid.* p. 721. Change of sculpture style *c.* 1500 is illustrated at Exeter, see E. K. Prideaux, *Building of Exeter*, pp. 137—139.

All through it was the character of a shop-art content to supply to sample as in the king-figures that were set in the niches of chancel screens and west fronts from 1375 for a hundred years. Saints and bishops witness to similar stock as the ordinary output of the imager's craft[1]. Only at Westminster in the first years of the sixteenth century did a somewhat fresher treatment appear in the figure-works of Henry VII's Chapel.

This is the latest, as indeed after Wells it is the largest, assemblage of English medieval imagery left. But how clearly do these rows of picturesque saintdom show medieval faith forgotten! Truly a Flemish Renaissance has been put by the side of the Italian which Henry VIII's sculptor, Torrigiano, was forging; emotional realism is in these smirks and attitudes no more than the mummer's action of a mystery play[2].

(*e*) Bourgeois Sculpture

The alabaster retables give us, better than the stone images, the sense of English fifteenth-century art. They are deliberately set forth in religious explanation of Christian creed, though the renderings aim only at spectacular vividness. Carved, undercut, and painted, the subject-panels were set in wood frames to make picture screens behind the altars. As an English trade and flourishing in the fifteenth century, they were exported to all Europe, and even accepted at Florence where Donatello was sculptor[3]. The wood-carvers too can be instanced as in their little novelettes enlivening latter-day style. At one time their story-telling is the Romance of the medieval moralities, the mermaids, dragons, wodehouses[4], griffins, and the dramatic absurdities of a scenic natural history. We have too life as it was

[1] *Ibid.* pp. 403 seq.; also S. Gardner, Pls. CXLVIII, CXLIX.

[2] *Ibid.* pp. 418, 419; see also W. R. Lethaby, *West. and King's Crafts.*

[3] Plate opp. p. 113. Framed alabaster retables are shown in author's *Med. Fig.-Sculp. in Eng.* pp. 463 seq.; also *English Medieval Alabaster Work*, 1913.

[4] "Wodehouses" are wild men, one of the fancies of the Bestiaries.

lived, wrought on the misericords of church stalls: the hunt and the chase, the beer-house broil, the humours of school, the habits of friars, the scolding wife. Very acute and spirited are often little grotesques of mouse, bat, weasel or owl, that were the commonplaces of country observation. As to legend or sacred story, if it could be made topical, then its representation becomes happy—as when the spies return with the enormous bunch of grapes from their survey of Canaan—or when Jonah is swallowed by the whale[1].

These were the special lines of local craft-production distributed from city centres. Nottingham was specially associated with the alabaster work: but during the fifteenth century a dozen other towns (and London among them) must have had their "alablaster-men" as they were called who took orders for "tables[2]." Another art-circulation of the same sort was that of the figure-carved fonts, which, first made at Norwich, would seem afterwards sent out, as were from many east-country centres[3] church-screens, stalls and misericords. The larger architectural sculptures and carvings must generally have been the work of building carpenters and masons. What chiefly throve in their art were Angels and Devils. There were the great trumpeting Archangels, dressed as in the Mystery plays in feathered costumes; on many ceilings the heavenly host was set buzzing like bees along the roof timbers[4]. Outside they hang like bats, from the corners of towers, or ranged in cornices they play every sort of instrument, happy joyous beings, as if they were performing in the village folk-plays and morris dances[5]. Equally irresponsible are the devils—in obscene caricature of the village pot-house characters. Such were the essential motives of the local homely

[1] Examples are given *Med. Fig.-Sculp. in Eng.* pp. 536 seq.

[2] Subject-panels. See author's *English Medieval Alabaster-work*, pp. 19, 20.

[3] Author's *Med. Fig.-Sculp. in Eng.* pp. 431 seq.; also S. Gardner, Pls. CLXXII, CLXXIII.

[4] *Ibid.* pp. 517—519.

[5] *Ibid.* pp. 520, 521.

crafts by which, east and west, north and south, Parish-church sculpture expressed the life and thought of the English fifteenth century[1].

(*f*) The Trades of Altar, Shrine, and Church-service

Moreover fifteenth-century churches were well stocked with art-works in the refined and costly executions of jewellers, metal-workers and embroiderers. The altar housings and deckings, the treasures of shrines and the other furniture of church-worship are known to us sometimes from entries in fabric rolls. Thus at Exeter we read that silver statues were made for the reredos. But precious work of this kind has long gone in England and the chief knowledge of what the churches contained remains to us in the state documents which record the spoliation of the larger monastic churches, such as the reports that were rendered to Cromwell, or in some actual descriptions of the dismantling itself. They tell us, for example, how the gold and jewels from St Thomas's shrine at Canterbury required 26 carts to remove them. For the furniture of parish-churches, there are the inventories which were made in Edward VI's reign, and we can so realize the extent of art-work that lay in the furnishing of a medieval church. One famous account has come down to us, as to the Cathedral of Durham, known as the "Rites of Durham": it is an inventory of regret as it were, made shortly after the Dissolution, and recounts all the furniture of the church and the ancient rule of its services. In museums can be seen some stray medieval

[1] As compared with Flanders, France, or Italy, the English arts of Henry VII's era were showing small capacity for the luxury of the sixteenth century; see the Paston letters. The insignificance of English art-production in respect of church furniture must be accepted when we note the extensive shop architectures of the fifteenth and sixteenth centuries, that are found in most continental cities. See as to France, Viollet le Duc, *Diction. de l'Architecture Française*, under the heading *Maison*, and for the Treasure of St Denis *Archaeologia*, 1914, 1915.

pieces, the débris recovered from the rubbish pits, into which the unholy hands of commissioners, covenanters and restorers have jettisoned them[1]. Most of the glass, in which the proficient art of the fifteenth-century glazier appeared, has been broken up or restored away, but enough remains to allow a fair estimate of its quality. Glass staining was a local craft, associated with certain capital cities, and the Winchester, York and London glaziers had their several craft-usages. In either case this craftsmanship was of extraordinary capacity whether as glazing, or as drawing[2]. As colourist the fifteenth-century glazier developed a fine if rather dry sense. His palette was that too of the fifteenth-century decorator, for it must be realized that all furniture and most wall surfaces were painted. The same golden browns, soft greys, full dark reds and greens can be seen in painters' finishings of stone and woodwork, in fonts, retables and parcloses, though not often now has such church-furniture come down to us unstripped[3].

We have this general reflection of an English bourgeois craft, that its arts were those of localized traditional skills which by long prescription attracted attention and custom. At times, no doubt, there were produced workers of special decorative genius, as the glazier, John Thornton of Coventry, who worked at York[4], or the "alablaster-men" so called of English cities whose customers were found all over Europe[5]. Of local trading were the carvers and painters of the Norfolk stone fonts, or those of wood screens and church-furniture, such as we see them at Ranworth and other east-country churches. With the screen

[1] The British Museum, Bloomsbury, and the Victoria and Albert Museum, Kensington, have specimens of enamels, and various church metal works.

[2] See H. Arnold, *Stained Glass*, Sections XIV, XVI.

[3] Coloured reproductions by E. W. Tristram can be studied at the Victoria and Albert Museum.

[4] *Ibid.* pp. 228 seq. [5] Plate opp. p. 113.

makers of the Devon churches there developed a picturesque speciality that lasted long into the sixteenth century[1]. But as regards religious expression, the fifteenth-century artist was content with canopied saints and conventional emblems—only escaping into the field of lively pantomime from some hint of a Mystery play. In the sixteenth century, however, there was to come widespread in Europe an art of anecdotal genre, which was the forerunner of the Northern Renaissance. As in the stone-carving of the Amiens quire-screen, or the thousand *curios* of the stalls there, so in the glass of the Doom at Fairford[2] are tales in line and colour—in expression just popular Punch and Judy shows—the last successes of the medieval crafts.

It was a perfunctory homage that the fifteenth-century building-mason paid to his sacred tradition. His Crucifixions and Annunciations once had the dignity of a creed, but now as much religious *aura* as a cusp or a flower-crocket. Still one moving interest survived to keep alive the pride of art, if not its sanctity. In state architecture the heraldry of kings and queens gave stonework a patent of nobility[3], and Angels were commissioned as the heralds of religion for aristocratic society. The combined formula of *angel and shield* in its decorous linking of Church and State, remained in art from Perpendicular tombs passing on to Tudor Porchways, and the Georgian Church Gallery.

(*g*) End of Church-building

To sum up the art reflection of the fifteenth-century life and thought, there were its two categories; (1) the state formality of academical theory, which had the stamp of officialism, and was expressed in royal foundations, in collegiate churches or chapels, as at Fotheringhay, at Windsor, at Eton, and King's College, Cambridge, or in the buildings of the king's ministers and

[1] S. Gardner, Pls. CLXIII, CLXIV.

[2] H. Arnold, *Stained Glass*, pp. 262, 263.

[3] *Ibid.* Pl. CL; also author's *Med. Fig.-Sculp. in Eng.* p. 522.

officers at Winchester; New College, Oxford; Bath Abbey[1], and Henry VII's Chapel, Westminster; (2) the Parish-church style of popular building—of collegiate chancels and chantry chapels, which took the forms of the official style, but used them with provincial variety and freedom in the service of trade-enriched classes. There was a thriving population establishing itself in civic rights, that claimed architecture of its own at Long Melford and Lavenham, at Norwich and Boston, at Hull and Newcastle in East England; at Taunton, Bristol, Wells and Cirencester in the west; at Coventry and Manchester in the midlands[2]. By the end of the century the political revolution had intervened: the King as a Renaissance despot was absorbing the three estates of the realm, Church, Lords and Commons. And so was closed the medieval era: for it was suppression of ideas, as well as of powers, when ecclesiastic and aristocratic interests ceased in church-building. Architectural art was being dedicated to domesticity in the fifteenth century. The Bishop's palace and the Lord's castle were become the living-rooms of an individual, and the public sense of church display was being displaced. It was all one evolution of European society that the printing-press was making religion and knowledge of private interpretation; that the hung picture superseded the church wall-painting; that engravings, antiques and bronzes interpreted culture; and that Henry appeared as the Renaissance despot patronizing Italian artists[3].

Such was the termination of the arts of church-building. In England it was abrupt in the quarrel of Henry VIII with Rome, in the assertion of his authority against Papal interference: for the incidents that marked it in England were the dissolution of monasteries, the suppression of guilds and chantries, and the

[1] For Bath Abbey see F. Bond, *Goth. Arch. in Eng.* p. 373.

[2] See back for illustrations, note 3, p. 130: for Lavenham see S. Gardner, Pl. LXI: for spires at Bristol, Coventry and Newcastle Figs. 45, 46, 52.

[3] See illustration of the new art, T. G. Jackson, *Renaissance*, Vol. 1.

destruction of what was called superstitious ornament. In some ten years was disestablished the whole of the church crafts that the centuries had specialized. Had this extinction of medieval culture proceeded, as it had gone on for a century or so, by the gradual decay of the sense of religious responsibility, then though shifted to new ideals Cathedrals and Churches might have come down to us with a preservation of their medieval antiquities much as Italian and Spanish churches show them. But the spasm of the English Reformation was one of violence to the ancient architectures: their widespread ruin marks the Elizabethan era as the English outcome of the Renaissance chaos. A conqueror in 1066 had established the monasteries and in their church-building had initiated for England its national art. A despot suppressed that medieval art when in the caprice of church reformation, monastic structures were laid waste and despoiled to augment the central authority of the state. Yet in the result the sudden and complete catastrophe begat a special and peculiarly national complexion in Elizabethan and Jacobean building. The manor-house was to be national in its rejection of ecclesiastic expression just as the church had been in acceptance of it at the Conquest. Each reflected the English position in the determination of its cultures. For English life and thought still found art in craftsmanship and would take neither French design for its medieval church-building, nor Italian for its Elizabethan house-building.

INDEX OF PLACES AND PRINCIPAL SUBJECTS

The references are dated approximately for the centuries in Roman numerals. The note-references are usually to published illustrations.

CAMBRIDGE: PRINTED BY
J. B. PEACE, M.A.,
AT THE UNIVERSITY PRESS